Quick & Easy
Pressure Cooker

Quick & Easy
Pressure Cooker

**More than 80 time-saving recipes
for soups, easy meals and desserts**

MURDOCH BOOKS

Contents

Introduction

It wasn't until 1939 that the first commercially produced modern saucepan-style pressure cookers became available. They featured an easy-to-close interlocking cover, and manufacturers were soon finding it hard to keep up with the demand for them due to their revolutionary time-saving advantages. Since then, the pressure cooker industry has continued to develop and improve the many styles and features available to the home cook.

Even though pressure cookers have always enjoyed popularity in Europe and Asia, they have experienced a resurgence in recent times in countries such as Australia and the United States. And the reasons are good ones.

- They are a great time saver: dishes that traditionally take hours to cook can be prepared in a pressure cooker in a fraction of the time, some up to 70 per cent faster.
- Pressure cookers are cost-saving — cheaper cuts of meat are most suited to pressure cooking, making it an economical way to cook.
- Nutritionally, pressure cookers also get a tick — the shorter cooking time needed means that generally more nutrients are retained, as well as flavour.
- Pressure cookers are great energy savers: because of the shorter cooking time involved, less energy is required during the cooking process — a great benefit in today's world.

How a pressure cooker works

Different models of pressure cookers can look quite different, and have different valves, regulators and locking systems, but they all work in a similar way.

Food is cooked using the pressure that is created by the steam trapped within it. Pressure cookers have a lid that can, when locked in place, completely seal the pot. When the liquid boils and creates steam, the steam is trapped in the pot, building up and increasing the pressure — and, in turn, increasing the boiling point of the liquid, as well as the temperature within the cooker.

The pressure of the trapped steam is measured in psi (pound of force per square inch). Check your instruction manual for the cooking pressure of your particular cooker. Some pressure cookers have both low and high settings. Generally 'low' will mean a psi of around 8, while 'high' will mean a psi of 12–15. A psi of 15 is the highest pressure a modern-day cooker will reach.

The higher the psi, the higher the pressure and temperature in the cooker, and the faster the food will cook. All our recipes specify either a 'low' or 'high' pressure setting when cooking. The pressure cookers used for testing the recipes in this book had a psi of 8 when set on low, and a psi of 15 when set on high.

In the past, pressure cookers have had a slightly infamous reputation for not being completely safe to use. Disasters involving the lid being forced off during cooking due to excess pressure building up, resulting in the contents of the pot being sprayed around the kitchen, are well known by many.

Thankfully, modern pressure cookers are much safer to use. They have a number of safety features, including inbuilt mechanisms that prevent the lid being removed before the pressure is completely released. They also have valves that will automatically release the pressure if it becomes too high.

Buying a pressure cooker

When it comes to size, pressure cookers generally range from around 4 litres (140 fl oz) to 10 litres (350 fl oz). A 4 litre (140 fl oz) cooker is ideal for singles or couples and smaller meals. The 6 litre (210 fl oz) cooker is a great size for most dishes serving 4–6 people. However, if you plan on braising lots of large cuts of meat or if you have a large family, consider an 8 litre (280 fl oz) or 10 litre (350 fl oz) cooker.

Consider the cooking pressure levels of the pressure cooker — some only have one psi level, while others offer at least two. Having more than one pressure level will give you greater control and flexibility when cooking various foods.

When choosing a pressure cooker, consider that the most durable are made of stainless steel with a 3-ply aluminium 'sandwich' base. Those with a heavy 'sandwich' base are good for browning meats before you add the liquid; they cook more evenly and will be less likely to scorch and develop 'hot spots'. It is also a good idea to choose a pressure cooker with heat-resistant handles.

Steaming baskets and trivets are good pressure cooker accessories, and many are sold with them. They are useful when steaming vegetables and cooking dishes that need to stay elevated above the water or sauce.

And remember, you get what you pay for as far as pressure control and ease of use goes.

Using your pressure cooker

Read your owner's manual carefully before you use your pressure cooker for the first time, and follow all the recommendations.

As with all cooking appliances, you will have to get to know your pressure cooker — for example, how quickly it cooks and how much liquid it needs. Note the results of the recipes you cook so you can adjust the cooking time and/or liquid content the next time if necessary.

In our recipes we have specified the size of the pressure cooker used. If using a different-sized cooker, you may need to alter the cooking time slightly.

Ingredients

Liquid is probably the most important ingredient when pressure cooking. As a general rule, your pressure cooker will need at least 250 ml (9 fl oz/1 cup) of liquid for the first 15 minutes of cooking, and an additional 150 ml (5 fl oz) for every extra 15 minutes (or part thereof) of cooking time. This is what all our recipes have been based on. However, pressure cookers do vary slightly and it is best to check your instruction manual to see if the manufacturer recommends a different amount.

More liquid can be added to these recipes, but never less — just make sure you don't fill the pot more than two-thirds full with combined food and liquid. If adding more liquid, remember that the final consistency of the dish will be slightly wetter.

If you are cooking ingredients that absorb liquid and expand during cooking — for example, grains such as rice and pearl barley, or dried pulses such as chickpeas, beans, lentils and split peas — don't fill your cooker more than half full.

Never use 'creamy' liquids such as milk, cream, coconut milk or coconut cream as the only liquid in the dish. Water or stock also needs to be added to dilute these ingredients, to reduce the risk of scorching during cooking.

Small amounts of yoghurt are fine to add to dishes before cooking under pressure, such as in a marinade, but generally yoghurt is best stirred through the dish at the end of cooking once the pressure has been released.

There are a few ingredients that don't cook well in a pressure cooker. These include pasta, dumplings and porridge. Dishes with flour also don't work well as they tend to scorch more easily.

If using flour, only use it in small quantities, such as for dusting meats before browning them.

Generally, it's a good idea to initially seal meats in a little oil until well browned before adding the liquid ingredients, as this helps develop a good flavour. For the same reason, vegetables used as a flavour base, such as onions, leeks and celery, as well as herbs and spices, are often best cooked in a little oil for a short while first.

Always prick foods with skins, such as sausages, before cooking. Also remember to cut an ingredient into similar-sized pieces so they will cook at the same rate.

Bringing the cooker up to pressure

If you have seared meat or other ingredients in the cooker, make sure you scrape up any bits clinging to the base of the pot. Adding a little wine, stock or water and simmering this for a short time while scraping the pot will help dislodge them. This will help prevent food scorching on the base of the cooker while pressure-cooking.

Always check the gasket or rubber seal and the valves in the lid before cooking. The gasket should be flexible, not damaged, and have no food sticking to it, otherwise the lid may not seal correctly. The valves should also be free of food, as lodged food can prevent them working properly, which means steam may not be regulated or released properly. Your manual will have further instructions about what to look for and how to maintain the gasket and valves.

Make sure your lid is correctly positioned and locked before you bring the cooker up to pressure. Your pressure cooker should be over a heat source that covers about one-third of the base of the pot. Use this heat source on high to bring the cooker to the desired pressure.

If using an electric stovetop, once the desired pressure is reached over high heat, transfer the pressure cooker immediately to a similar-sized burner set on low. This way the pressure can be stabilised immediately without waiting for the electric burner to reduce to low.

If using a gas stovetop, never let the flames come up around the side of the pot as this may damage it.

It can take as little as 1 minute or as long as 15 minutes for a cooker to come up to pressure, depending on your particular pressure cooker model, what you are cooking and how much liquid the dish contains. Our 'cooking time' at the beginning of our recipes doesn't include bringing the cooker up to pressure or depressuring it, due to this variation in time.

Maintaining the pressure

Once the correct pressure is reached, as registered by the valve or regulator on the lid, turn the heat down to the lowest possible setting to stabilise the pressure. There should only be a gentle hissing coming from the valve, if at all. If the hissing is more forceful, reduce the heat even further to reduce the steam being released and to stabilise the pressure.

Always use a timer — timing is crucial when using a pressure cooker. Start timing as soon as the specified pressure is reached. This is easy to tell with models that have inbuilt timers, as the alarm will sound. For those that don't, start timing from the moment that there is a constant and stable jet of steam being released through the valve and once you have stabilised the pressure.

Keep an eye on the pressure and stove heat at all times, as they need to be kept consistent and well regulated for the best results.

Be prepared to adjust the heat if needed during cooking. After the first few uses of your pressure cooker, you will quickly work out which burner on your stovetop is most suitable.

A heat diffuser is a very handy accessory when getting to know your pressure cooker. If your cooker doesn't have a heavy base, or you have an unpredictable heat source or one that can't be set low enough to stabilise the pressure, food may scorch on the base of the cooker. A heat diffuser, when placed between the heat and the cooker, will spread the heat evenly over the bottom of the pot and reduce the intensity of the heat, helping to prevent scorching. It is also very helpful to use when cooking rice, grains and pulses to stop these sticking to the pot and scorching.

You may have to play around with the diffuser a little to get the heat level correct, but once you've worked it out the results will be great.

Releasing the pressure

There are two ways of releasing the steam and, in turn, the pressure from your cooker — the 'natural' method, and the automatic or 'quick' release method. The recipes in this book will specify which one to use.

- **Natural release method:** To release the pressure naturally, simply remove the cooker from the heat and set it aside until the pressure is released. Generally this method is recommended for dishes such as curries, casseroles, stews and braises using cheaper cuts of meat, as well as larger, whole cuts of meat, as they will often toughen if the pressure is released too quickly. This method is also recommended for beans and potatoes as it helps them hold onto their skins.

- **Automatic or 'quick' release method:** Some pressure cookers have an automatic 'quick' release method. Check your manual and, if yours does, simply follow the instructions given. If it doesn't, you can still quickly release the steam, and therefore the pressure, by running cold water over the top of the cooker (away from vents and the regulator) until all the pressure is released — it won't take long. This method is good to use when adding extra ingredients during the cooking process or for those foods that easily overcook, such as fish and vegetables.

You may need to add different ingredients at different times during cooking, depending on the time they take to cook. If so, release the pressure using the 'quick' release method, stir in the additional ingredients, lock the lid back in place and then continue with the recipe.

This is well worth doing to retain the best flavour and texture of individual ingredients.

Finishing a dish

When removing the lid from the cooker once the pressure has been released, lift it up facing away from you, to protect you from any escaping steam that may burn.

If you feel your dish has too much liquid at the end of the cooking time (using different pressure cooker models will often affect the liquid content), you can thicken the sauce by simmering it, uncovered, in the pot until the desired consistency and flavour is achieved. Alternatively, you can blend a little plain (all-purpose) flour or cornflour (cornstarch) with a little of the cooking liquid before returning it to the pot, and then simmer it for a few minutes while stirring.

Cleaning and storing your pressure cooker

Make sure you read and follow the manufacturer's care instructions for your pressure cooker.

Wash the gasket separately by hand in warm soapy water. The lid shouldn't be immersed in water, as the safety valves can be damaged. The pot is best washed by hand and dried immediately, although some can be washed in a dishwasher — check your manual for specific recommendations.

Store your cooker with the lid off. Never lock it in place, as the gasket can be damaged and any odours will be trapped inside. If the lid is locked in place and there is any moisture trapped inside, it will be nearly impossible to remove the lid.

Key points to remember

- Read your owner's manual carefully before you use your pressure cooker for the first time.

- Never fill your pressure cooker more than two-thirds full with combined food and liquid.

- The 'cooking time' at the beginning of our recipes doesn't include bringing the cooker up to pressure or depressuring it.

- There should only be a gentle hissing coming from the valve, if at all. If the hissing is more forceful, reduce the heat.

- Always use a timer — timing is crucial when using a pressure cooker.

- When removing the lid from the cooker, lift it up facing away from you, to protect you from any escaping steam.

- Store your cooker with the lid off. Never lock it in place.

Cooking rice in a pressure cooker

Put your unrinsed rice and water or stock in a 6 litre (210 fl oz) pressure cooker. Lock the lid in place and bring it to the specified pressure over high heat. Once the pressure is reached, reduce the heat to stabilise the pressure, then cook for the specified time. Release the pressure and carefully remove the lid, then stir the rice with a fork to separate the grains. Lock the lid back in place and stand for 5 minutes before serving. These quantities are sufficient to serve 4–6 people.

Rice	Quantity	Water or stock quantity	Pressure level	Cooking time	Release method
White medium-grain	220 g (7¾ oz/ 1 cup)	350 ml (12 fl oz)	low	7 minutes	natural
White long-grain	200 g (7 oz/1 cup)	350 ml (12 fl oz)	low	6 minutes	natural
Jasmine	200 g (7 oz/1 cup)	350 ml (12 fl oz)	low	6 minutes	natural
Basmati	200 g (7 oz/1 cup)	350 ml (12 fl oz)	low	6 minutes	natural
Brown medium-grain	220 g (7¾ oz/ 1 cup)	375 ml (13 fl oz/ 1½ cups)	low	17 minutes	natural
Brown long-grain	200 g (7 oz/1 cup)	500 ml (17 fl oz/ 2 cups)	low	23 minutes	natural

Note: All times are based on 8 psi for 'low' pressure and 15 psi for 'high' pressure.

Cooking dried pulses in a pressure cooker

Rinse the pulses. If needed, soak the pulses in plenty of water for at least 8 hours or overnight. Drain well, then place the drained pulses and specified quantity of water or stock in a 6 litre (210 fl oz) pressure cooker. Lock the lid in place and bring to the specified pressure over high heat. Once the pressure is reached, reduce the heat to stabilise the pressure, then cook for the specified time. Release the pressure and carefully remove the lid, then drain the pulses of any residual liquid.

Pulse	Quantity	Soak overnight	Water or stock quantity	Pressure level	Cooking time	Release method
Red kidney beans	190 g (6¾ oz/ 1 cup)	yes	750 ml (26 fl oz)	high	20 minutes	natural
Cannellini beans	200 g (7 oz/ 1 cup)	yes	750 ml (26 fl oz)	high	8 minutes	natural
Black-eyed beans	185 g (6½ oz/ 1 cup)	yes	750 ml (26 fl oz)	high	8 minutes	natural
Chickpeas	200 g (7 oz/ 1 cup)	yes	750 ml (26 fl oz)	high	10 minutes	natural
Pearl barley	200 g (7 oz/ 1 cup)	yes	1 litre (35 fl oz)	high	15 minutes	natural
Puy lentils	210 g (7½ oz/ 1 cup)	no	1 litre (35 fl oz)	low	18 minutes	natural
Green/ brown lentils	215 g (7½ oz/ 1 cup)	no	500 ml (17 fl oz)	low	12 minutes	natural

Note: All times are based on 8 psi for 'low' pressure and 15 psi for 'high' pressure.

STOCKS

Chicken stock

Preparation time 10 minutes • **Cooking time** 30 minutes • **Makes** 1.5 litres (52 fl oz/6 cups)

1 kg (2 lb 4 oz) chicken pieces, such as a
meatless carcass, necks and/or wings
1 brown onion, chopped
1 leek, pale section only, rinsed and sliced
1 carrot, thickly sliced
2 celery stalks, sliced
100 g (3½ oz) button mushrooms,
coarsely chopped

1 lemon peel strip, about 1 cm (½ inch) x 5 cm
(2 inches), white pith removed
3 flat-leaf (Italian) parsley stalks
2 large thyme sprigs
1 bay leaf
8 black peppercorns

1 Place all the ingredients in an 8 litre (280 fl oz) pressure cooker and add 2 litres (70 fl oz/8 cups) cold water. Lock the lid in place and bring the cooker to high pressure over high heat. Once high pressure is reached, reduce the heat to stabilise the pressure and cook for 30 minutes.

2 Remove the cooker from the heat and release the pressure using the natural release method. Remove the lid carefully.

3 Strain the stock through a sieve lined with muslin (cheesecloth); discard any solids. Refrigerate overnight, then skim any fat from the surface. Taste and season with salt and freshly ground black pepper.

NOTE: The stock will keep in an airtight container in the refrigerator for up to 3 days, or in the freezer for up to 1 month.

Beef stock

Preparation time 10 minutes • **Cooking time** 30 minutes • **Makes** 1.5 litres (52 fl oz/6 cups)

1 kg (2 lb 4 oz) meaty beef or veal bones
  (see Notes)
1 brown onion, chopped
1 leek, pale section only, rinsed and chopped
1 carrot, thickly sliced
125 g (4½ oz) button mushrooms,
  coarsely chopped

2 celery stalks, sliced
1 tomato, coarsely chopped
3 flat-leaf (Italian) parsley stalks
2 large thyme sprigs
1 bay leaf
8 black peppercorns

1 Place all the ingredients in an 8 litre (280 fl oz) pressure cooker and add 2 litres (70 fl oz/8 cups) cold water. Lock the lid in place and bring the cooker to high pressure over high heat. Once high pressure is reached, reduce the heat to stabilise the pressure and cook for 30 minutes.

2 Remove the cooker from the heat and release the pressure using the natural release method. Remove the lid carefully.

3 Strain the stock through a sieve lined with muslin (cheesecloth); discard any solids. Refrigerate overnight, then skim any fat from the surface. Taste and season with salt and freshly ground black pepper.

NOTES: For a richer and more intensely flavoured stock, brown the bones all over, in batches, in a little oil in the pressure cooker pot over medium heat. Wipe out the pan, return all the bones to the cooker and continue as above.

The stock will keep in an airtight container in the refrigerator for up to 3 days, or in the freezer for up to 1 month.

Vegetable stock

Preparation time 10 minutes • **Cooking time** 30 minutes • **Makes** 1.75 litres (61 fl oz/7 cups)

1 brown onion, chopped
1 leek, pale section only, rinsed and chopped
1 carrot, thickly sliced
2 celery stalks, chopped
1 tomato, quartered
125 g (4½ oz) button mushrooms, coarsely
   chopped

1 lemon peel strip, about 2 cm (¾ inch) wide,
   white pith removed
3 flat-leaf (Italian) parsley stalks
2 large thyme sprigs
1 bay leaf
8 black peppercorns
1 teaspoon sea salt flakes

1 Place all the ingredients in an 8 litre (280 fl oz) pressure cooker and add 1.8 litres (63 fl oz) cold water. Lock the lid in place and bring the cooker to high pressure over high heat. Once high pressure is reached, reduce the heat to stabilise the pressure and cook for 30 minutes.

2 Remove the cooker from the heat and release the pressure using the natural release method. Remove the lid carefully.

3 Strain the stock through a sieve lined with muslin (cheesecloth). Discard any solids.

NOTE: The stock will keep in an airtight container in the refrigerator for up to 3 days, or in the freezer for up to 1 month.

Fish stock

Preparation time 10 minutes • **Cooking time** 20 minutes • **Makes** 2 litres (70 fl oz/8 cups)

1.25 kg (2 lb 12 oz) white fish bones and heads,
   gills removed
1 brown onion, coarsely chopped
1 leek, pale section only, rinsed and chopped
1 carrot, thickly sliced

1 celery stalk, coarsely chopped
2 flat-leaf (Italian) parsley stalks
1 large thyme sprig
1 bay leaf
8 black peppercorns

1 Thoroughly rinse all the fish bones and heads to remove any trace of blood. Place all the ingredients in an 8 litre (280 fl oz) pressure cooker and add 1.8 litres (63 fl oz) cold water. Lock the lid in place and bring the cooker to high pressure over high heat. Once high pressure is reached, reduce the heat to stabilise the pressure and cook for 20 minutes.

2 Remove the cooker from the heat and release the pressure using the natural release method. Remove the lid carefully.

3 Strain the stock through a sieve lined with muslin (cheesecloth). Discard any solids.

NOTE: The stock will keep for up to 3 days in the refrigerator, or up to 1 month in the freezer.

Soups

Lamb and barley soup with peas

Preparation time 10 minutes • **Cooking time** 22 minutes • **Serves** 4

4 (about 800 g/1 lb 12 oz) lamb forequarter
  or neck chops
1 leek, pale section only, coarsely chopped
2 carrots, cut into 2 cm (¾ inch) thick rounds
2 garlic cloves, chopped
1 brown onion, chopped
200 g (7 oz/1 cup) pearl barley, rinsed
  and drained

1 tablespoon fennel seeds
6 thyme sprigs (tied with kitchen string)
1 litre (35 fl oz/4 cups) good-quality purchased
  or homemade chicken stock (see page 14)
1 tablespoon worcestershire sauce
140 g (5 oz/1 cup) frozen peas
¼ cup flat-leaf (Italian) parsley leaves, chopped
crusty bread, to serve

1 Place all the soup ingredients, except the peas and parsley, in an 8 litre (280 fl oz) pressure cooker. Add 500 ml (17 fl oz/2 cups) water and season with salt and freshly ground black pepper.

2 Lock the lid in place and bring the cooker to high pressure over high heat. Once high pressure is reached, reduce the heat to stabilise the pressure and cook for 20 minutes, or until the lamb and barley are tender. Remove the cooker from the heat and release the pressure using the natural release method. Remove the lid carefully.

3 Discard the thyme. Remove the lamb from the cooker and allow to cool slightly. When cool enough to handle, shred the meat and return it to the cooker. Discard the bones.

4 Add the peas and parsley to the cooker and simmer, uncovered, over medium heat for 1–2 minutes, or until the peas are heated through.

5 Taste the soup and season as needed. Serve with crusty bread.

Spiced carrot soup with coriander and cashew paste

Preparation time 20 minutes • **Cooking time** 10 minutes • **Serves** 6–8

2 tablespoons olive oil
1 red onion, diced
1 garlic clove, chopped
1 teaspoon cumin seeds
1 teaspoon sweet paprika
1 teaspoon garam masala (see Note)
3 small red chillies, seeded and chopped
1.5 litres (52 fl oz/6 cups) good-quality purchased or homemade chicken stock (see page 14)
6 large carrots, peeled and chopped
1 kg (2 lb 4 oz) sweet potatoes, peeled and cut into 1 cm (½ inch) chunks

2 large all-purpose potatoes, peeled and cut into 1 cm (½ inch) chunks
300 ml (10½ fl oz) coconut cream
chargrilled naan bread, to serve

CORIANDER AND CASHEW PASTE
40 g (1½ oz/¼ cup) roasted unsalted cashew nuts
1 cup (30 g/1 oz) coriander (cilantro) leaves
1 small garlic clove, halved
60 ml (2 fl oz/¼ cup) coconut milk
1 tablespoon lime juice, or to taste
1½ tablespoons olive oil

---

1 To make the coriander and cashew paste, place the cashews, coriander, garlic, coconut milk and lime juice in a small food processor and process until the nuts are finely chopped. With the motor running, gradually add the oil in a thin steady stream until well combined. Cover and set aside.

2 Heat the oil in an 8 litre (280 fl oz) pressure cooker over medium–high heat and cook the onion and garlic, stirring often, for 3–4 minutes, or until the onion has softened. Stir in the spices and chilli and cook for a further 30–60 seconds, or until aromatic. Immediately stir in the stock, then add the vegetables.

3 Lock the lid in place and bring the cooker to high pressure over high heat. Once high pressure is reached, reduce the heat to stabilise the pressure and cook for 5 minutes, or until the vegetables are very tender. Remove the cooker from the heat and release the pressure using the quick release method. Remove the lid carefully.

4 Using a stick blender, purée the soup until smooth. (Alternatively, transfer the mixture to a food processor or blender, in batches if necessary, and purée until smooth. Return the soup to the cooker.)

5 Stir in the coconut cream, then season to taste with salt and freshly ground black pepper. Reheat over low heat if necessary.

6 Serve with a swirl of the cashew paste, and chargrilled naan bread on the side.

NOTE: Garam masala is a blend of ground spices — typically including pepper, mace, cloves, cumin, coriander, cinnamon, cardamom and fennel — that is widely used in Indian cooking to enhance spicy dishes. It is available from supermarkets.

Thai-style pumpkin soup

Preparation time 25 minutes • **Cooking time** 6 minutes • **Serves** 6 as a main or 12 as a starter

2 (about 3 kg/6 lb 12 oz) butternut pumpkins
 (squash), peeled, seeded and chopped
1 brown onion, finely chopped
4 makrut (kaffir lime) leaves, torn
1 lemongrass stem, bruised
2 teaspoons finely grated fresh ginger
1 tablespoon fish sauce
270 ml (9½ fl oz) tin coconut cream

1 tablespoon Thai red curry paste
1 litre (35 fl oz/4 cups) good-quality purchased
 or homemade chicken stock (see page 14)
 or vegetable stock (see page 18)
2 teaspoons lime juice
1 long red chilli, seeded and finely chopped
coriander (cilantro) leaves, to garnish

---

1 Place the pumpkin, onion, lime leaves, lemongrass, ginger and fish sauce in an 8 litre (280 fl oz) pressure cooker. Reserve 2 tablespoons of the coconut cream, then mix the curry paste with the remaining coconut cream until smooth. Pour the mixture into the cooker, then pour in the stock and gently mix together.

2 Lock the lid in place and bring the cooker to high pressure over high heat. Once high pressure is reached, reduce the heat to stabilise the pressure and cook for 6 minutes, or until the pumpkin is very tender. Remove the cooker from the heat and release the pressure using the quick release method. Remove the lid carefully. Discard the lemongrass and lime leaves.

3 Using a stick blender, purée the soup until smooth. (Alternatively, transfer the mixture to a food processor or blender, in batches if necessary, and purée until smooth. Return the soup to the cooker.)

4 Stir in the lime juice and reheat over low heat if necessary.

5 Serve the soup drizzled with the reserved coconut cream, and garnished with the chilli and some coriander leaves.

NOTE: This soup can be frozen. Allow the soup to cool, then transfer to an airtight container. Label and date the container and freeze for up to 6 months.

Tunisian chickpea and silverbeet soup

Preparation time 10 minutes • **Cooking time** 12 minutes • **Serves** 4

1 bunch (about 900 g/2 lb) silverbeet
   (Swiss chard)
2 tablespoons olive oil
1 brown onion, finely sliced
1 teaspoon ground white pepper
1 teaspoon freshly grated nutmeg
1/2 teaspoon ground cumin
1/4 teaspoon ground cloves

1/4 teaspoon ground cinnamon
2 x 400 g (14 oz) tins chickpeas, rinsed and drained
750 ml (26 fl oz/3 cups) good-quality purchased
   or homemade chicken stock (see page 14)
   or vegetable stock (see page 18)
Greek-style yoghurt, to serve
crusty bread, to serve
lemon wedges, to serve

1 Wash the silverbeet leaves well and shake dry. Remove the stem below the leaf and discard. Slice the leaves into ribbons 2 cm (3/4 inch) thick and set aside.

2 Heat the oil in a 6 litre (210 fl oz) pressure cooker over medium–high heat and cook the onion, stirring occasionally, for 3 minutes, or until it starts to colour. Reduce the heat to low and cook for another 5 minutes, or until the onion is soft.

3 Add the pepper, nutmeg, cumin, cloves and cinnamon and cook, stirring, for 30 seconds, or until aromatic. Add the chickpeas, stirring to coat them well in the spices. Stir in the stock and silverbeet.

4 Lock the lid in place and bring to low pressure over high heat. Once low pressure is reached, reduce the heat to stabilise the pressure and cook for 3 minutes, or until the silverbeet is just tender.

5 Remove the cooker from the heat and release the pressure using the natural release method. Remove the lid carefully.

6 Transfer one-third of the soup to a food processor and process until almost smooth. Return to the cooker with the remaining soup. Season to taste with salt and freshly ground black pepper and reheat over low heat if necessary.

7 Ladle the soup into serving bowls and top with a small dollop of yoghurt. Serve with crusty bread and lemon wedges.

Hearty chicken noodle soup

Preparation time 15 minutes • **Cooking time** 7 minutes • **Serves** 4–6

125 g (4½ oz) dried rice stick noodles (see Notes)
3 (about 600 g/1 lb 5 oz) skinless chicken
  breast fillets
750 ml (26 fl oz/3 cups) good-quality purchased
  or homemade chicken stock (see page 14)
2 celery stalks, cut into 1.5 cm (⅝ inch) chunks
1 brown onion, cut into 1.5 cm (⅝ inch) chunks
2 carrots, cut into 1 cm (½ inch) chunks

1 parsnip, peeled and cut into 1 cm
  (½ inch) chunks
2 cm (¾ inch) piece of fresh ginger
3 black peppercorns
2 zucchini (courgettes), cut into 1 cm
  (½ inch) chunks
finely chopped flat-leaf (Italian) parsley
  leaves, to garnish

1 Place the noodles in a heatproof bowl. Cover with boiling water and leave to soak for 10 minutes, or until softened. Drain well and set aside.

2 Meanwhile, place the chicken, stock, celery, onion, carrot, parsnip, ginger, peppercorns and 250 ml (9 fl oz/1 cup) water in a 6 litre (210 fl oz) pressure cooker. Lock the lid in place and bring the cooker to low pressure over high heat. Once low pressure is reached, reduce the heat to stabilise the pressure and cook for 4 minutes, or until the chicken is just tender.

3 Remove the cooker from the heat and release the pressure using the natural release method. Remove the lid carefully.

4 Remove the chicken from the pressure cooker with a slotted spoon and allow to cool slightly. Shred the chicken when cool enough to handle.

5 Meanwhile, place the pressure cooker over medium heat, add the zucchini and simmer gently for 2 minutes, or until just tender. Discard the ginger and season the soup to taste with salt and freshly ground black pepper.

6 Add the noodles (see Notes) and shredded chicken to the soup and cook over medium heat for 1 minute, or until just warmed through.

7 Serve the soup sprinkled with parsley.

NOTES: Instead of sprinkling parsley over the finished soup, try some chopped basil or coriander (cilantro) leaves. You can also stir some chopped chilli through for a spicy kick.

If preparing the soup ahead, don't add the noodles until reheating the soup.

Without the noodles, the soup can be frozen in an airtight container for up to 3 months.

Curried chicken and peanut soup

Preparation time 30 minutes • **Cooking time** 8 minutes • **Serves** 4

250 g (9 oz) dried rice vermicelli noodles
2 tablespoons fish sauce
2 garlic cloves, crushed
1 tablespoon lime juice
1 tablespoon brown sugar
2 small red chillies, seeded if desired,
   then finely chopped
1 kg (2 lb 4 oz) skinless chicken thigh fillets,
   trimmed
270 ml (9½ fl oz) tin coconut cream
chopped salted roasted peanuts, to garnish
coriander (cilantro) sprigs, to garnish

SPICE PASTE
⅓ cup chopped coriander (cilantro) leaves
   and stems
½ small white onion, chopped
1 teaspoon finely grated fresh galangal (see Note)
1 teaspoon ground turmeric
1 teaspoon ground coriander
2 tablespoons roasted salted peanuts
1½ tablespoons peanut oil

1 Place the noodles in a heatproof bowl. Cover with boiling water and leave to soak for 10 minutes, or until softened. Drain well and set aside.

2 Meanwhile, combine the fish sauce, garlic, lime juice, sugar, chilli and 750 ml (26 fl oz/3 cups) water in an 8 litre (280 fl oz) pressure cooker. Stir until the sugar has dissolved, then add the chicken.

3 Lock the lid in place and bring the cooker to high pressure over high heat. Once high pressure is reached, reduce the heat to stabilise the pressure and cook for 5 minutes, or until the chicken is tender.

4 Meanwhile, place all the spice paste ingredients in a small food processor or blender. Process to a smooth paste and set aside.

5 Remove the cooker from the heat and release the pressure using the natural release method. Remove the lid carefully. Remove the chicken from the pressure cooker with a slotted spoon and allow to cool slightly. Pour the liquid from the cooker through a sieve into a bowl and reserve. Shred the chicken when cool enough to handle and set aside.

6 Wipe out the cooker and place over medium heat. Add the curry paste and cook, uncovered, for 2–3 minutes, or until aromatic, stirring regularly. Add the coconut cream and the reserved cooking liquid and bring to a gentle simmer. Remove the cooker from the heat and stir in the shredded chicken to just warm through.

7 Divide the noodles among serving bowls and ladle the soup over the top. Garnish with chopped peanuts and coriander sprigs and serve.

NOTE: Galangal is a fragrant rhizome belonging to the ginger family. It resembles ginger but is slightly pink, with a thin skin that should be peeled before using. It is widely used in South East Asian cooking and is available from Asian grocers and good greengrocers.

Mexican meatball soup

Preparation time 40 minutes (+ 30 minutes resting) • **Cooking time** 18 minutes • **Serves** 6

2 tablespoons olive oil

1 brown onion, finely chopped

1 garlic clove, chopped

1 teaspoon ground cumin

250 ml (9 fl oz/1 cup) purchased Mexican salsa

400 g (14 oz) tin chopped tomatoes

1 litre (35 fl oz/4 cups) good-quality purchased
or homemade beef stock (see page 17)

400 g (14 oz) tin red kidney beans, rinsed and
drained

1/2 cup coriander (cilantro) leaves, chopped

50 g (1³/4 oz/1/2 cup) coarsely grated cheddar cheese

sour cream, to serve

corn chips, to serve (optional)

MEATBALLS

500 g (1 lb 2 oz) minced (ground) beef

50 g (1³/4 oz/1/2 cup) coarsely grated cheddar
cheese

30 g (1 oz/1/2 cup, lightly packed) fresh
breadcrumbs

2 egg yolks

1 garlic clove, chopped

1/3 cup coriander (cilantro) leaves, chopped

2 tablespoons lime juice

1/2 teaspoon chilli powder, or to taste

1 teaspoon dried oregano

1 teaspoon ground cumin

1 Combine all the meatball ingredients in a large mixing bowl and season well with salt and freshly ground black pepper. Using moist hands, roll heaped tablespoons of the mixture into balls. Place on a tray, cover with plastic wrap and refrigerate for 30 minutes, or until required.

2 Heat 1½ tablespoons of the oil in an 8 litre (280 fl oz) pressure cooker over medium–high heat and cook the meatballs in two batches, turning regularly, for 3–4 minutes, or until golden. Set aside.

3 Reduce the heat to medium and add the remaining oil and the onion to the cooker. Cook for 5 minutes, or until softened, then add the garlic and cumin and cook, stirring constantly, for 1 minute. Stir in the salsa, tomatoes, stock and kidney beans until well combined. Add the meatballs.

4 Lock the lid in place and bring the cooker to low pressure over high heat. Once low pressure is reached, reduce the heat to stabilise the pressure and cook for 4 minutes, or until the meatballs are cooked through. Remove the cooker from the heat and release the pressure using the natural release method. Remove the lid carefully.

5 Stir in the coriander and season to taste. Divide the soup and meatballs among warm serving bowls. Scatter with the cheese, add a dollop of sour cream and serve with corn chips, if desired.

Prawn laksa lemak

Preparation time 25 minutes • **Cooking time** 15 minutes • **Serves** 4

250 g (9 oz) dried rice stick noodles
½ small red onion, chopped
1 lemongrass stem, pale section only, chopped
finely grated zest of 1 lime
¼ cup coriander (cilantro) leaves, chopped,
   plus extra sprigs, to garnish
90 g (3¼ oz/⅓ cup) purchased laksa paste
1 tablespoon peanut oil
1 tablespoon grated palm sugar (jaggery),
   or brown sugar

1 tablespoon fish sauce
270 ml (9½ fl oz) tin coconut cream
24 (about 600 g/1 lb 5 oz) raw king prawns
   (shrimp), peeled and deveined, leaving the
   tails intact and reserving the shells
90 g (3¼ oz/¾ cup) bean sprouts, tails trimmed
Thai basil leaves, to garnish
sambal oelek, to serve (see Note)

1 Place the noodles in a heatproof bowl. Cover with boiling water and leave to soak for 10 minutes, or until softened. Drain well and set aside.

2 Meanwhile, place the onion, lemongrass, lime zest and coriander in a small food processor and process until combined. Add the laksa paste and process to a smooth paste.

3 Heat the oil in a 6 litre (210 fl oz) pressure cooker over medium heat. Add the laksa paste mixture and cook, stirring, for 3–4 minutes, or until aromatic. Add the sugar and stir for 1 minute. Pour in the fish sauce, 60 ml (2 fl oz/¼ cup) of the coconut cream and 750 ml (26 fl oz/3 cups) water. Stir well, then add the reserved prawn shells.

4 Lock the lid in place and bring the cooker to high pressure over high heat. Once high pressure is reached, reduce the heat to stabilise the pressure and cook for 7 minutes. Remove the cooker from the heat and release the pressure using the quick release method. Remove the lid carefully.

5 Strain the cooking liquid and discard any solids. Wash out the cooker, then return the strained stock to the pot and place over medium heat. Stir in the remaining coconut cream and bring to a simmer. Add the prawns and simmer, uncovered, for 2–3 minutes, or until pink and just cooked through. Season to taste with salt.

6 Divide the noodles among deep serving bowls, then ladle the laksa over the noodles. Top with the bean sprouts, garnish with coriander and Thai basil and serve with sambal oelek.

NOTE: Sambal oelek is a spicy condiment made from ground chillies. It is widely used in Indonesian and Malaysian cooking and is available from the Asian section of supermarkets.

Cream of parsnip soup

Preparation time 20 minutes • **Cooking time** 13 minutes • **Serves** 4–6 (as a starter)

1 kg (2 lb 4 oz) parsnips, peeled and chopped
200 g (7 oz) all-purpose potatoes, peeled
  and chopped
1 granny smith apple, peeled, cored and
  chopped
1 brown onion, finely chopped

1 garlic clove, chopped
750 ml (26 fl oz/3 cups) good-quality purchased
  or homemade chicken stock (see page 14)
a pinch of saffron threads
250 ml (9 fl oz/1 cup) pouring (whipping) cream
snipped chives, to serve

1 Place the parsnip, potato, apple, onion, garlic, stock and saffron in a 6 litre (210 fl oz) pressure cooker.

2 Lock the lid into place and bring the cooker to high pressure over high heat. Once high pressure is reached, reduce the heat to stabilise the pressure and cook for 8 minutes, or until the parsnip and potato are tender.

3 Remove the cooker from the heat and release the pressure using the quick release method. Remove the lid carefully.

4 Purée the soup until smooth, using a stick blender. (Alternatively, transfer the mixture to a food processor or blender, in batches if necessary, and purée until smooth. Return the soup to the cooker.)

5 Stir in the cream, then season to taste with salt and freshly ground black pepper. Place the cooker over medium–high heat and cook, uncovered, for a further 5 minutes, or until the soup has thickened slightly, stirring occasionally.

6 Serve sprinkled with chives and plenty of freshly ground black pepper.

NOTES: For a vegetarian soup, replace the chicken stock with vegetable stock (see page 18).
  For a sensational dinner-party starter, serve this soup topped with pan-fried scallops.
  If you find the soup is a little fibrous from the woody section of the parsnip, pass the soup through a fine sieve after puréeing it.

Chunky pea and ham soup

Preparation time 10 minutes • **Cooking time** 45 minutes • **Serves** 4–6

1 tablespoon olive oil
1 brown onion, finely chopped
2 garlic cloves, finely chopped
2 teaspoons dried thyme
1 teaspoon dried oregano
2 bay leaves
500 ml (17 fl oz/2 cups) good-quality purchased
   or homemade chicken stock (see page 14)

1 smoked ham hock, about 600 g (1 lb 5 oz)
2 carrots, peeled and chopped
2 celery stalks, sliced
300 g (10½ oz/1⅓ cups) split green peas,
   rinsed and drained
¼ cup mint leaves, coarsely chopped, plus
   extra, to garnish
crusty bread, to serve (optional)

1 Heat the oil in an 8 litre (280 fl oz) pressure cooker over medium heat and cook the onion, garlic, thyme, oregano and bay leaves for 3 minutes, or until softened. Add the stock, ham hock and 1 litre (35 fl oz/4 cups) water.

2 Lock the lid in place and bring the cooker to high pressure over high heat. Once high pressure is reached, reduce the heat to stabilise the pressure and cook for 20 minutes. Remove the cooker from the heat and release the pressure using the quick release method. Remove the lid carefully.

3 Add the carrot, celery and split peas, season with freshly ground black pepper, replace the lid immediately and lock in place. Bring the cooker back to high pressure over high heat. Once high

pressure is reached, reduce the heat to stabilise the pressure and cook for a further 22 minutes, or until the peas are tender and the meat is falling off the bone.

4 Remove the cooker from the heat and release the pressure using the natural release method. Remove the lid carefully.

5 Transfer the ham hock to a plate and set aside until cool enough to handle. Cut the meat into small chunks and return it to the soup.

6 Gently reheat the soup. Stir in the mint, then ladle into serving bowls. Sprinkle with extra mint and serve with crusty bread, if desired.

Moroccan lentil soup

Preparation time 10 minutes • **Cooking time** 16 minutes • **Serves** 4–6

1 tablespoon olive oil
1 large brown onion, finely chopped
2 garlic cloves, finely chopped
2 teaspoons ground cumin
2 teaspoons ground coriander
½ teaspoon ground turmeric
½ teaspoon paprika
½ teaspoon ground ginger
400 g (14 oz) tin chopped tomatoes

225 g (8 oz) dried green or brown lentils, rinsed and drained
2 tablespoons chopped flat-leaf (Italian) parsley leaves, plus extra, to garnish
1 litre (35 fl oz/4 cups) good-quality purchased or homemade chicken stock (see page 14)
lime wedges, to serve
crusty bread, to serve

1 Heat the oil in a 6 litre (210 fl oz) pressure cooker over medium heat and cook the onion and garlic for 3 minutes, or until the onion is softened. Add all the spices and cook, stirring, for 1 minute, or until aromatic.

2 Add the tomatoes, lentils, parsley and stock and season with freshly ground black pepper. Lock the lid in place and bring the cooker to high pressure over high heat. Once high pressure is reached, reduce the heat to stabilise the pressure and cook for 12 minutes, or until the lentils are tender.

3 Remove the cooker from the heat and release the pressure using the natural release method. Remove the lid carefully.

4 Taste and adjust the seasoning, if required. Ladle the soup into serving bowls. Sprinkle with extra parsley and serve with lime wedges and crusty bread.

Cauliflower and cumin soup

Preparation time 10 minutes • **Cooking time** 16 minutes • **Serves** 6

2 tablespoons butter
1 large brown onion, coarsely chopped
2 garlic cloves, chopped
2 (about 750 g/1 lb 10 oz each) small cauliflowers,
    cores removed, coarsely chopped
1 tablespoon ground cumin
½ teaspoon ground cinnamon

250 ml (9 fl oz/1 cup) good-quality purchased
    or homemade chicken stock (see page 14)
250 ml (9 fl oz/1 cup) milk
185 ml (6 fl oz/¾ cup) coconut milk
chilli powder, for sprinkling
2 tablespoons pine nuts, toasted

1 Melt the butter in a 6 litre (210 fl oz) pressure cooker over medium heat and cook the onion and garlic with a pinch of salt for 5 minutes, stirring occasionally, until the onion is softened. Add the cauliflower, cumin and cinnamon and cook, stirring occasionally, for a further 5 minutes, or until the cauliflower starts to soften.

2 Add the stock and 250 ml (9 fl oz/1 cup) water to the cooker. Lock the lid in place and bring the cooker to high pressure over high heat. Once high pressure is reached, reduce the heat to stabilise the pressure and cook for 4 minutes, or until the cauliflower is very tender.

3 Remove the cooker from the heat and release the pressure using the natural release method. Remove the lid carefully.

4 Stir in the milk and coconut milk and purée the soup with a stick blender. (Alternatively, transfer the mixture to a food processor or blender, in batches if necessary, and purée until smooth. Return the soup to the cooker.)

5 Place the cooker over medium heat and simmer, uncovered, for 2 minutes. Season the soup with salt and freshly ground black pepper.

6 Ladle the soup into serving bowls. Serve sprinkled with chilli powder, some more freshly ground black pepper and the pine nuts.

NOTE: If the soup is too thick after blending, stir in an extra 60–125 ml (2–4 fl oz/¼–½ cup) chicken stock.

Mains

CHICKEN

Chicken, pumpkin and honey braise

Preparation time 10 minutes • **Cooking time** 6 minutes • **Serves** 4–6

250 ml (9 fl oz/1 cup) good-quality purchased
  or homemade chicken stock (see page 14)
90 g (3¼ oz/¼ cup) honey
1 tablespoon dijon mustard
1 large brown onion, chopped
1 kg (2 lb 4 oz) skinless chicken thigh fillets

750 g (1 lb 10 oz) butternut pumpkin (squash),
  peeled, seeded and chopped into 2.5 cm
  (1 inch) chunks
⅓ cup chopped flat-leaf (Italian) parsley leaves
cooked basmati rice (see page 12), to serve

1 Place the stock, honey and mustard in a 6 litre (210 fl oz) pressure cooker and stir over low heat to combine.

2 Add the onion, chicken, pumpkin and half the parsley to the cooker. Season with freshly ground black pepper.

3 Lock the lid in place and bring the cooker to high pressure over high heat. Once high pressure is reached, reduce the heat to stabilise the pressure and cook for 6 minutes, or until the chicken and pumpkin are just cooked through.

4 Remove the cooker from the heat and release the pressure using the natural release method. Remove the lid carefully. Taste and adjust the seasoning, if necessary.

5 Serve the chicken and pumpkin braise on a bed of rice, sprinkled with the remaining parsley.

Mexican chicken

Preparation time 25 minutes • **Cooking time** 18 minutes • **Serves** 4

1 teaspoon chilli flakes
2 teaspoons ground cumin
¼ teaspoon ground cinnamon
60 ml (2 fl oz/¼ cup) olive oil
4 small (about 1.25 kg/2 lb 12 oz) chicken
   marylands
1 red onion, coarsely chopped
2 fresh green jalapeño chillies, finely chopped
4 garlic cloves, finely chopped
200 g (7 oz) jar hot taco sauce
250 ml (9 fl oz/1 cup) good-quality purchased
   or homemade chicken stock (see page 14)

1 red capsicum (pepper), cut into 2 cm
   (¾ inch) chunks
1 green capsicum (pepper), cut into 2 cm
   (¾ inch) chunks
2 corn cobs, silks and husks removed,
   then cut into thick rounds
100 g (3½ oz) whole black olives
coriander (cilantro) leaves, to garnish
cooked white long-grain rice (see page 12),
   to serve
85 g (3 oz/⅓ cup) sour cream
warmed flour tortillas, to serve (optional)

1 Combine the chilli flakes, cumin, cinnamon and 2 tablespoons of the oil in a large bowl. Add the chicken pieces and toss to coat. Rub the spice mixture into the chicken skin with your fingers, making sure the chicken is entirely covered. Season with salt.

2 Heat the remaining oil in an 8 litre (280 fl oz) pressure cooker over medium heat and cook the chicken pieces in two batches for 5 minutes, or until well browned on all sides, adding a little more oil if necessary. Remove from the cooker and set aside.

3 Add the onion, jalapeño chilli, garlic, taco sauce, stock, capsicum and corn to the cooker, scraping the base of the pot. Return the chicken to the pot and stir to coat in the sauce.

4 Lock the lid in place and bring the cooker to high pressure over high heat. Once high pressure is reached, reduce the heat to stabilise the pressure and cook for 8 minutes, or until the chicken is moist and tender.

5 Remove the cooker from the heat and release the pressure using the natural release method. Remove the lid carefully. Skim the excess oil from the surface of the sauce.

6 Stir the olives through the chicken mixture. Divide among serving plates and garnish with coriander. Serve with rice and sour cream, and warmed flour tortillas if desired.

Cajun chicken stew

Preparation time 10 minutes • **Cooking time** 7 minutes • **Serves** 6

1.5 kg (3 lb 5 oz) skinless chicken thigh fillets,
   trimmed and cut in half
1½ tablespoons hot cajun seasoning (see Note)
60 ml (2 fl oz/¼ cup) olive oil
60 ml (2 fl oz/¼ cup) good-quality purchased
   or homemade chicken stock (see page 14)
400 g (14 oz) tin chopped tomatoes
1 red capsicum (pepper), cut into 1 cm (½ inch)
   chunks

2 celery stalks, thinly sliced
1 large brown onion, diced
60 ml (2 fl oz/¼ cup) worcestershire sauce
3 bay leaves
1 teaspoon sugar
1 garlic clove, crushed
1 teaspoon freshly ground black pepper
cooked basmati rice (see page 12), to serve

1 Place all the ingredients except the rice in a 6 litre (210 fl oz) pressure cooker. Stir until well combined.

2 Lock the lid in place and bring the cooker to high pressure over medium–high heat. Once high pressure is reached, reduce the heat to stabilise the pressure and cook for 7 minutes, or until the chicken is tender.

3 Remove the cooker from the heat and release the pressure using the natural release method. Remove the lid carefully.

4 Serve the stew on a bed of rice.

NOTE: You'll find hot cajun seasoning in the spice aisle of your supermarket.

Spanish chicken

Preparation time 20 minutes • **Cooking time** 7 minutes • **Serves** 4

750 g (1 lb 10 oz) skinless chicken thigh
  fillets (about 6), trimmed and cut into
  4 cm (1½ inch) chunks
2 (about 260 g/9¼ oz) chorizo sausages,
  cut into 2 cm (¾ inch) slices
1 red onion, chopped
4 garlic cloves, finely chopped
1 green chilli, seeded and finely chopped
2 teaspoons smoked paprika (see Note)

1 teaspoon dried oregano
400 g (14 oz) tin chopped tomatoes
250 ml (9 fl oz/1 cup) good-quality purchased
  or homemade chicken stock (see page 14)
140 g (5 oz/1 cup) frozen peas
100 g (3½ oz) bottled roasted red capsicum
  (pepper) pieces, thinly sliced
crusty bread, to serve

1 Place the chicken in a 6 litre (210 fl oz) pressure cooker with the chorizo, onion, garlic, chilli, paprika, oregano, tomatoes and stock. Season with salt and freshly ground black pepper and mix well.

2 Lock the lid in place and bring the cooker to high pressure over high heat. Once high pressure is reached, reduce the heat to stabilise the pressure and cook for 6 minutes, or until the chicken is tender.

3 Remove the cooker from the heat and release the pressure using the natural release method. Remove the lid carefully.

4 Add the peas and capsicum to the cooker and stir gently to combine. Place the cooker over medium–high heat and cook, uncovered, for 1 minute, or until the peas are bright green.

5 Ladle the mixture into serving bowls and serve with crusty bread.

NOTE: A signature spice in Spanish cuisine, smoked paprika is made from capsicums (peppers) that have been slowly smoked, then ground to a fine powder. It is widely available, but if you don't have any, you can use sweet paprika instead.

Red cooked chicken

Preparation time 20 minutes • **Cooking time** 10 minutes • **Serves** 8

500 ml (17 fl oz/2 cups) good-quality purchased
   or homemade chicken stock (see page 14)
250 ml (9 fl oz/1 cup) light soy sauce
45 g (1½ oz/¼ cup) brown sugar
60 ml (2 fl oz/¼ cup) Chinese rice wine or
   medium–sweet sherry
125 ml (4 fl oz/½ cup) hoisin sauce
2.4 kg (5 lb 6 oz) chicken pieces
4 cm (1½ inch) piece of fresh ginger, peeled
   and thinly sliced

1½ teaspoons fennel seeds
1 cinnamon stick
2 star anise
3 orange peel strips, each about 2 cm (¾ inch)
   wide, white pith removed, plus some extra
   thin orange zest strips, to garnish
2 spring onions (scallions), green section cut
   into long thin strips
cooked jasmine rice (see page 12), to serve
steamed bok choy (pak choy), to serve

---

1 Place the stock, soy sauce, sugar, Chinese rice wine and hoisin sauce in a 6 litre (210 fl oz) pressure cooker over low heat and cook, stirring, until the sugar has dissolved. Add the chicken, ginger, fennel seeds, cinnamon stick, star anise and thick orange peel strips.

2 Lock the lid in place and bring the cooker to high pressure over high heat. Once high pressure is reached, reduce the heat to stabilise the pressure and cook for 8 minutes, or until the chicken is just tender. Remove the cooker from the heat and release the pressure using the natural release method. Remove the lid carefully.

3 Skim as much excess fat from the surface of the cooking liquid as possible. Discard the cinnamon stick, star anise and thick orange peel strips.

4 Divide the chicken among wide shallow serving bowls, then ladle the broth over the top. Garnish with thin orange zest and spring onion strips. Serve with rice and bok choy.

African chicken

Preparation time 20 minutes • **Cooking time** 29 minutes • **Serves** 4

1 tablespoon olive oil
4 (about 800 g/1 lb 12 oz) chicken drumsticks
2 (about 500 g/1 lb 2 oz) skinless chicken thigh
   fillets, trimmed and halved
2 brown onions, thinly sliced
2 tablespoons Moroccan spice mix (see Note)
2 garlic cloves, crushed
2 tablespoons tomato paste (concentrated purée)
400 g (14 oz) tin chopped tomatoes
250 ml (9 fl oz/1 cup) good-quality purchased
   or homemade chicken stock (see page 14)

coriander (cilantro) sprigs, to garnish
lemon cheeks, to serve

HERBED COUSCOUS
280 g (10 oz/1½ cups) instant couscous
½ cup coriander (cilantro) leaves, chopped
1 tablespoon olive oil

1 Heat the oil in an 8 litre (280 fl oz) pressure cooker over medium–high heat and cook the chicken pieces in two batches for 5 minutes, or until well browned on all sides. Remove from the cooker and set aside. Discard all but 1 tablespoon of the oil in the cooker.

2 Reduce the heat to medium. Add the onion to the cooker and cook, stirring occasionally, for 8 minutes, or until softened and starting to brown. Stir in the Moroccan spice mix and cook, stirring, for 30 seconds, or until aromatic. Add the garlic and tomato paste and cook, stirring, for 1 minute. Add the tomatoes and stock and simmer for 2 minutes, scraping the base of the pot. Return the chicken to the cooker and stir well.

3 Lock the lid in place and bring the cooker to high pressure over high heat. Once high pressure is reached, reduce the heat to stabilise the pressure and cook for 7 minutes, or until the chicken is tender. Remove the cooker from the heat and release the pressure using the natural release method. Remove the lid carefully. Taste and season with salt and freshly ground black pepper if desired.

4 Meanwhile, place the couscous in a heatproof bowl and pour in 375 ml (13 fl oz/1½ cups) boiling water. Stir with a fork for 10 seconds. Cover with a tea towel (dish towel) and leave to stand for 3 minutes, or until the liquid has been absorbed. Stir the grains with a fork to break up any lumps, then stir in the coriander and oil. Season to taste with salt and freshly ground black pepper.

5 Spoon the couscous into wide shallow serving bowls. Arrange the chicken pieces on top and drizzle with the sauce. Garnish with coriander and serve with lemon cheeks.

NOTE: You'll find Moroccan spice mix in the spice aisle of your supermarket.

Chicken Madeira with mushrooms

Preparation time 20 minutes • **Cooking time** 12–18 minutes • **Serves** 6

20 g (¾ oz) butter
250 g (9 oz) button mushrooms, halved, or
  quartered if large
1 kg (2 lb 4 oz) skinless chicken thigh fillets,
  trimmed and halved
1 leek, pale section only, rinsed, three-quarters
  chopped and one-quarter cut into thin strips
2 teaspoons chopped rosemary leaves
2 bay leaves

80 ml (2½ fl oz/⅓ cup) good-quality purchased
  or homemade chicken stock (see page 14)
125 ml (4 fl oz/½ cup) Madeira (see Note)
125 ml (4 fl oz/½ cup) pouring (whipping) cream
mashed potato, to serve
chopped flat-leaf (Italian) parsley leaves,
  to garnish
thin lemon zest strips, to garnish

1 Melt the butter in a 6 litre (210 fl oz) pressure cooker over medium heat. Add the mushrooms and cook, stirring occasionally, for 6 minutes, or until golden on all sides. Remove from the cooker and set aside.

2 Season the chicken with salt and freshly ground black pepper and place in the cooker. Add the chopped leek, rosemary, bay leaves, stock, Madeira and cream and gently combine.

3 Lock the lid in place and bring the cooker to high pressure over high heat. Once high pressure is reached, reduce the heat to stabilise the pressure and cook for 6 minutes, or until the chicken is

tender. Remove the cooker from the heat and release the pressure using the natural release method. Remove the lid carefully.

4 Stir in the mushrooms and season to taste. If a thicker sauce is desired, remove the chicken and simmer the sauce for 5–6 minutes.

5 Serve the chicken on a bed of mashed potato, drizzled with the sauce and garnished with parsley, lemon zest and the leek strips.

NOTE: Madeira is a fortified wine from the Portuguese island of Madeira. It will add a subtle sweetness to this dish.

Saffron chicken with fennel and green olive tapénade

Preparation time 30 minutes • **Cooking time** 18 minutes • **Serves** 4–6

2½ tablespoons olive oil
1.6 kg (3 lb 8 oz) chicken pieces
375 ml (13 fl oz/1½ cups) good-quality purchased
  or homemade chicken stock (see page 14)
a large pinch of saffron threads (see Note)
2 garlic cloves, thinly sliced
finely grated zest of 1 lemon, plus the juice
8 (about 500 g/1 lb 2 oz) small new potatoes,
  halved
1 fennel bulb, trimmed and cut into wedges
2 leeks, pale section only, trimmed and cut into
  2 cm (¾ inch) thick rounds
2 carrots, cut into 1 cm (½ inch) thick rounds

2 celery stalks, cut into 2 cm (¾ inch) chunks
  on the diagonal
⅓ cup flat-leaf (Italian) parsley leaves, chopped
crusty bread, to serve

GREEN OLIVE TAPÉNADE
85 g (3 oz/½ cup) pimento-stuffed green olives
1 garlic clove
1 tablespoon capers in brine, rinsed and drained
2 drained anchovy fillets
⅓ cup flat-leaf (Italian) parsley leaves
2 tablespoons olive oil

1 To make the green olive tapénade, coarsely chop the olives, garlic, capers, anchovies and parsley in a small food processor. Season with freshly ground black pepper, add the oil and blend until combined. Cover and set aside until required.

2 Heat the oil in an 8 litre (280 fl oz) pressure cooker over medium–high heat and cook the chicken pieces in two batches for 5 minutes, or until well browned on all sides. Remove from the cooker and set aside. Discard any oil in the cooker.

3 Return all the chicken pieces to the cooker. Combine the stock, saffron, garlic, lemon juice and lemon zest in a bowl and pour over the chicken. Pile the potatoes on top of the chicken.

4 Lock the lid in place and bring the cooker to high pressure over high heat. Once high pressure is reached, reduce the heat to stabilise the pressure and cook for 3 minutes. Remove the cooker from the heat and release the pressure using the quick release method. Remove the lid carefully.

5 Add the fennel, leek, carrot and celery, replace the lid immediately and lock in place. Bring the cooker back to high pressure over high heat. Once high pressure is reached, reduce the heat to stabilise the pressure and cook for 5 minutes, or until the chicken and vegetables are tender.

6 Remove the cooker from the heat and release the pressure using the natural release method. Remove the lid carefully.

7 Stir the parsley through the stew, then divide among warm deep bowls. Top with a spoonful of the tapénade and serve with crusty bread.

NOTE: Although saffron is a costly spice, a little goes a very long way and nothing else compares to its warm, mellow flavour or the lovely golden colour it imparts. You can buy saffron in powdered form or as threads; the threads (which are actually the dried stamens of a type of crocus flower) give the best flavour.

BEEF

Beef short ribs with molasses, bourbon and thyme

Preparation time 20 minutes • **Cooking time** 40 minutes • **Serves** 4

1½ tablespoons olive oil

1.5 kg (3 lb 5 oz) beef short ribs,
  separated into single ribs

700 ml (24 fl oz) jar tomato passata
  (puréed tomatoes)

125 ml (4 fl oz/½ cup) red wine

90 g (3¼ oz/¼ cup) molasses

60 ml (2 fl oz/¼ cup) bourbon

1 tablespoon dijon mustard

1 tablespoon worcestershire sauce

2 brown onions, chopped

2 carrots, cut in half lengthways,
  then cut into 1 cm (½ inch) slices

4 garlic cloves, chopped

3 thyme sprigs, plus extra, to garnish

1 bay leaf

1 teaspoon freshly ground black pepper

½ teaspoon chilli flakes

cooked white long-grain rice (see page 12),
  to serve

1 Heat the oil in an 8 litre (280 fl oz) pressure cooker over medium–high heat and cook the ribs in two batches for 3–4 minutes on each side, or until well browned on all sides, turning regularly. Remove from the cooker and set aside. Discard the oil from the cooker.

2 Place the passata, wine, molasses, bourbon, mustard, worcestershire sauce and 60 ml (2 fl oz/¼ cup) water in the cooker over low heat and simmer for 1–2 minutes, scraping the base of the pot. Return the ribs to the cooker with the onion, carrot, garlic, thyme, bay leaf, pepper and chilli flakes and stir well.

3 Lock the lid in place and bring the cooker to high pressure over high heat. Once high pressure is reached, reduce the heat to stabilise the pressure and cook for 25 minutes, or until the ribs are very tender. Remove the cooker from the heat and release the pressure using the natural release method. Remove the lid carefully.

4 Skim any fat from the surface of the sauce. Discard the bay leaf and thyme and check the seasoning. Garnish with extra thyme leaves and serve with rice.

Indonesian beef stew

Preparation time 15 minutes • **Cooking time** 35 minutes • **Serves** 4–6

1 kg (2 lb 4 oz) beef chuck steak, trimmed
   and cut into 4 cm (1½ inch) chunks
1 brown onion, chopped
2 carrots, coarsely grated
2 garlic cloves, finely chopped
375 ml (13 fl oz/1½ cups) good-quality purchased
   or homemade beef stock (see page 17)
1 teaspoon sesame oil

2 tablespoons kecap manis (see Note)
1 tablespoon light soy sauce
1 tablespoon tomato sauce (ketchup)
1 tablespoon sweet chilli sauce
coriander (cilantro) leaves, to garnish
fried Asian shallots, to serve (optional)
cooked basmati rice (see page 12),
   to serve

1 Place the beef in a 6 litre (210 fl oz) pressure cooker. Add the onion, carrot, garlic, stock, sesame oil, kecap manis, soy sauce, tomato sauce and sweet chilli sauce and stir to combine.

2 Lock the lid in place and bring the cooker to high pressure over high heat. Once high pressure is reached, reduce the heat to stabilise the pressure and cook for 30 minutes, or until the beef is very tender. Remove the cooker from the heat and release the pressure using the natural release method. Remove the lid carefully.

3 Place the cooker back over medium heat and simmer, uncovered, for 5 minutes, or until the sauce has thickened slightly. Reduce the sauce further if desired.

4 Ladle the stew into wide shallow serving bowls. Garnish with coriander and fried Asian shallots, if desired, and serve with rice.

NOTE: Kecap manis is a thick, sweet soy sauce from Indonesia. It is available from the Asian section of supermarkets and from Asian grocery stores.

Vietnamese beef brisket

Preparation time 20 minutes • **Cooking time** 27 minutes • **Serves** 4

1.5 kg (3 lb 5 oz) beef brisket, trimmed of excess fat and cut into 3 cm (1¼ inch) chunks
2 lemongrass stems, pale section only, chopped
2 long red chillies, seeded and thinly sliced on the diagonal
10 cm (4 inch) piece of fresh ginger, cut into thin matchsticks
60 ml (2 fl oz/¼ cup) soy sauce
2 tablespoons fish sauce

2 carrots, cut on the diagonal into 1 cm (½ inch) thick slices
2 tablespoons lime juice
cooked jasmine rice (see page 12), to serve
125 g (4½ oz) cherry tomatoes, quartered
90 g (3¼ oz/¾ cup) bean sprouts, tails trimmed
Vietnamese mint leaves, to garnish
small basil leaves, to garnish

1 Combine the beef, lemongrass, chilli, ginger, soy sauce, fish sauce and 125 ml (4 fl oz/½ cup) water in a 6 litre (210 fl oz) pressure cooker.

2 Lock the lid in place and bring the cooker to high pressure over high heat. Once high pressure is reached, reduce the heat to stabilise the pressure and cook for 25 minutes, or until the beef is moist and tender. Remove the cooker from the heat and release the pressure using the quick release method. Remove the lid carefully.

3 Add the carrot, replace the lid immediately and lock in place. Bring the cooker back to high pressure over high heat. Once high pressure is reached, reduce the heat to stabilise the pressure and cook for 2 minutes, or until the carrot is tender.

4 Remove the cooker from the heat and release the pressure using the natural release method. Remove the lid carefully. Skim any fat from the surface of the sauce, then stir in the lime juice.

5 Serve the beef on a bed of rice, drizzled with the sauce and garnished with the cherry tomatoes, bean sprouts, mint and basil.

NOTE: This dish may also be served with rice noodles. Simply cover 300 g (10½ oz) dried rice noodles with boiling water and allow them to soak for 5 minutes, or until softened, then drain and rinse. Before serving with the beef brisket, stir some chopped coriander (cilantro) leaves through the noodles if desired.

Boeuf en daube

Preparation time 30 minutes • **Cooking time** 48 minutes • **Serves** 4–6

2 tablespoons olive oil
1 kg (2 lb 4 oz) beef chuck steak, trimmed
    and cut into 3 cm (1¼ inch) chunks
8 (about 400 g/14 oz) pickling onions, peeled
    and halved
150 g (5½ oz) bacon slices, cut into 1.5 cm
    (⅝ inch) pieces
2 garlic cloves, crushed
1 tablespoon tomato paste (concentrated purée)
125 ml (4 fl oz/½ cup) good-quality purchased or
    homemade beef stock (see page 17)

125 ml (4 fl oz/½ cup) red wine
1 tablespoon chopped thyme leaves
2 bay leaves
1 carrot, chopped
1 celery stalk, cut into 1.5 cm (⅝ inch) chunks
cooked short pasta, such as casarecce, trofie
    or pasta twists, to serve
chopped flat-leaf (Italian) parsley leaves,
    to serve
crusty bread, to serve

1 Heat half the oil in an 8 litre (280 fl oz) pressure cooker over medium–high heat and cook the beef in three batches for 5 minutes, or until well browned on all sides, adding a little more oil if necessary. Remove from the cooker and set aside.

2 Heat the remaining oil in the cooker over medium–high heat and cook the onions and bacon for 5 minutes, or until the onions are golden, stirring occasionally. Add the garlic and cook, stirring, for a further 1 minute. Add the tomato paste, stock, wine, thyme and bay leaves and simmer for 2 minutes, scraping the base of the pot. Return the beef to the cooker and stir well.

3 Lock the lid in place and bring the cooker to high pressure over high heat. Once high pressure is reached, reduce the heat to stabilise the pressure and cook for 20 minutes, or until the beef is almost tender. Remove the cooker from the heat and release the pressure using the quick release method. Remove the lid carefully.

4 Add the carrot and celery, replace the lid immediately and lock into place. Bring the cooker back to high pressure over high heat. Once high pressure is reached, reduce the heat to stabilise the pressure and cook for 5 minutes, or until the beef and vegetables are tender.

5 Remove the cooker from the heat and release the pressure using the natural release method. Remove the lid carefully. Season the mixture to taste with salt and freshly ground black pepper.

6 Serve the beef on a bed of pasta, drizzled with the sauce and sprinkled with parsley, and with crusty bread on the side.

NOTE: Boeuf en daube is a classic French braise that usually requires several hours of slow cooking. It takes its name from the deep covered pottery casserole dish, *daubière*, in which it is traditionally cooked.

Creamy beef with tomatoes

Preparation time 15 minutes • **Cooking time** 27 minutes • **Serves** 6

60 ml (2 fl oz/¼ cup) good-quality purchased
or homemade chicken stock (see page 14)
60 ml (2 fl oz/¼ cup) white wine
1½ tablespoons tomato paste
(concentrated purée)
2 teaspoons sweet paprika
1 teaspoon salt
½ teaspoon freshly ground black pepper
1.5 kg (3 lb 5 oz) beef chuck steak, trimmed
and cut into 3 cm (1¼ inch) chunks

1 brown onion, finely chopped
2 garlic cloves, crushed
500 g (1 lb 2 oz) cherry tomatoes, halved
100 g (3½ oz/½ cup) semi-dried (sun-blushed)
tomatoes, chopped
125 g (4½ oz/½ cup) sour cream
prepared couscous, to serve
small basil leaves, to garnish

1 Combine the stock, wine and tomato paste in a 6 litre (210 fl oz) pressure cooker. Mix the paprika, salt and pepper in a large bowl, add the beef and toss until evenly coated. Transfer to the cooker and add the onion, garlic and all the tomatoes. Gently mix together.

2 Lock the lid in place and bring the cooker to high pressure over high heat. Once high pressure is reached, reduce the heat to stabilise the pressure and cook for 25 minutes, or until the beef is tender.

3 Remove the cooker from the heat and release the pressure using the natural release method. Remove the lid carefully.

4 Add the sour cream and stir gently to combine. Place the cooker back over medium heat and cook, uncovered, and stirring occasionally, for 2 minutes, or until just heated through (do not boil).

5 Serve the beef mixture on a bed of couscous, garnished with basil leaves.

Beef ragù

Preparation time 25 minutes • **Cooking time** 15–25 minutes • **Serves** 6

RAGÙ
1 kg (2 lb 4 oz) minced (ground) beef
400 g (14 oz) tin chopped tomatoes
250 ml (9 fl oz/1 cup) tomato passata (puréed
   tomatoes) or pasta sauce
125 ml (4 fl oz/½ cup) red wine
2 carrots, finely diced
2 brown onions, finely diced
2 celery stalks, finely diced
2 tablespoons pesto
2 tablespoons tomato paste (concentrated purée)

4 garlic cloves, crushed
1 teaspoon chilli flakes (optional)
½ teaspoon dried oregano
1 rosemary sprig
1 thyme sprig

cooked pasta tubes, such as penne
   or rigatoni, to serve
finely chopped flat-leaf (Italian) parsley
   leaves, to serve
finely grated parmesan cheese, to serve

1 Place all the ragù ingredients in a 6 litre (210 fl oz) pressure cooker and mix to combine. Lock the lid in place and bring the cooker to high pressure over high heat. Once high pressure is reached, reduce the heat to stabilise the pressure and cook for 15 minutes.

2 Remove the cooker from the heat and release the pressure using the natural release method. Remove the lid carefully.

3 If necessary, place the pot back over medium heat and simmer, uncovered, for 5–10 minutes, stirring regularly, until the liquid has reduced to a good sauce consistency.

4 Serve the ragù on a bed of pasta, sprinkled with a little parsley and parmesan.

NOTE: The ragù can be frozen if desired. Allow it to cool to room temperature, then transfer to an airtight container and freeze for up to 3 months. This recipe can also be made using minced (ground) lamb.

Spiced beef with prunes and silverbeet

Preparation time 20 minutes • **Cooking time** 45 minutes • **Serves** 6

60 ml (2 fl oz/¼ cup) olive oil
1.25 kg (2 lb 12 oz) beef chuck steak, trimmed
   and cut into 4 cm (1½ inch) chunks
2 brown onions, chopped
2 garlic cloves, crushed
1 teaspoon mixed (pumpkin pie) spice
1 teaspoon ground cinnamon
2 teaspoons ground turmeric
1 teaspoon ground cumin
500 ml (17 fl oz/2 cups) good-quality purchased
   or homemade chicken stock (see page 14)
   or veal stock

105 g (3½ oz/½ cup) pitted prunes, chopped
1 ripe tomato, chopped
3 (about 500 g/1 lb 2 oz) all-purpose potatoes,
   peeled and cut into 2 cm (¾ inch) chunks
2 carrots, cut into 2 cm (¾ inch) chunks
350 g (12 oz) silverbeet (Swiss chard), stems
   removed, leaves washed, dried and chopped
coriander (cilantro) leaves, to garnish
plain yoghurt, to serve

1 Heat 2 tablespoons of the oil in an 8 litre (280 fl oz) pressure cooker over medium–high heat and cook the beef in three batches for 4 minutes, or until well browned on all sides, turning often. Remove from the cooker and set aside.

2 Reduce the heat to medium and heat the remaining oil in the cooker. Add the onion and garlic and cook for 3–4 minutes, or until the onion starts to soften. Stir in the spices and cook for 1 minute, or until aromatic, stirring constantly. Add the stock and simmer for 2 minutes, scraping the base of the pot. Return the beef to the cooker with the prunes and tomato and stir well.

3 Lock the lid in place and bring the cooker to high pressure over high heat. Once high pressure is reached, reduce the heat to stabilise the pressure and cook for 20 minutes, or until the beef is almost tender. Remove the cooker from the heat and release the pressure using the quick release method. Remove the lid carefully.

4 Add the potato, carrot and silverbeet to the cooker, replace the lid immediately and lock into place. Bring the cooker back to high pressure over high heat. Once high pressure is reached, reduce the heat to stabilise the pressure and cook for 6 minutes, or until the beef and vegetables are tender.

5 Remove the cooker from the heat and release the pressure using the natural release method. Remove the lid carefully.

6 Season to taste with salt and freshly ground black pepper, then spoon the mixture into warmed bowls. Garnish with coriander leaves, drizzle with yoghurt and serve.

Chilli con carne

Preparation time 10 minutes • **Cooking time** 22 minutes • **Serves** 4

1 tablespoon olive oil
1 chorizo sausage, halved lengthways and sliced
1 large brown onion, diced
300 g (10½ oz) minced (ground) beef
2 garlic cloves, crushed
3 teaspoons ground cumin
2 teaspoons ground coriander
3 x 420 g (15 oz) tins red kidney beans,
  rinsed and drained

400 g (14 oz) tin chopped tomatoes
1 teaspoon dried oregano
1 avocado, chopped
½ cup coriander (cilantro) leaves, chopped
warmed flour tortillas, to serve
sour cream, to serve

1 Heat the oil in a 6 litre (210 fl oz) pressure cooker over medium–high heat and cook the chorizo for 2 minutes, or until browned. Add the onion and cook for 3 minutes, stirring, until softened.

2 Add the beef and cook for 2 minutes, or until it changes colour, breaking it up with a wooden spoon. Stir in the garlic and spices and cook until aromatic. Stir in the kidney beans, tomatoes, oregano and 125 ml (4 fl oz/½ cup) water. Season to taste with salt and freshly ground black pepper.

3 Lock the lid in place and bring the cooker to high pressure over high heat. Once high pressure is reached, reduce the heat to stabilise the pressure and cook for 15 minutes.

4 Remove the cooker from the heat and release the pressure using the natural release method. Remove the lid carefully.

5 Divide the chilli con carne, avocado and coriander among the tortillas. Spoon some sour cream over, roll up tightly and serve.

NOTES: You can replace the tinned beans with 190 g (6¾ oz/1 cup) dried red kidney beans. Follow the cooking instructions on page 13.

If you like your chilli con carne hot, add 1 teaspoon chilli flakes when adding the oregano, or serve the finished dish with Tabasco sauce.

The chilli con carne can be frozen in an airtight container for up to 3 months.

VEAL

Veal with tarragon-lemon cream and broad beans

Preparation time 20 minutes • **Cooking time** 33 minutes • **Serves** 6

1.25 kg (2 lb 12 oz) veal stewing steak
  (such as blade), untrimmed, cut into
  3 cm (1¼ inch) chunks
¼ teaspoon freshly ground black pepper
1 teaspoon salt
1½ tablespoons wholegrain mustard
80 ml (2½ fl oz/⅓ cup) white wine
185 ml (6 fl oz/¾ cup) good-quality purchased
  or homemade chicken stock (see page 14)
1 brown onion, very finely chopped

2 garlic cloves, crushed
2 tarragon sprigs, plus extra chopped leaves,
  to garnish
1 teaspoon finely grated lemon zest, plus some
  extra thin lemon zest strips, to garnish
60 ml (2 fl oz/¼ cup) pouring (whipping) cream
375 g (13 oz/2⅓ cups) frozen or podded fresh
  broad (fava) beans, peeled (see Note)
mashed potato, to serve

1 Place the veal, pepper and salt in a 6 litre (210 fl oz) pressure cooker and toss until evenly coated. Mix the mustard with the wine and add to the cooker, along with the stock, onion, garlic and tarragon sprigs. Gently mix together.

2 Lock the lid in place and bring the cooker to high pressure over high heat. Once high pressure is reached, reduce the heat to stabilise the pressure and cook for 25 minutes, or until the veal is tender.

3 Remove the cooker from the heat and release the pressure using the natural release method. Remove the lid carefully.

4 Remove the tarragon sprigs and stir in the lemon zest and cream. Place the cooker over medium–high heat and simmer, uncovered, for a further 2 minutes, or until the sauce has thickened slightly. Stir in the broad beans and cook for a further 1 minute for frozen beans or 3–5 minutes for fresh beans, or until just cooked through.

5 Serve with mashed potato, garnished with extra chopped tarragon and lemon zest strips.

NOTE: To peel frozen and fresh broad beans, first blanch them in boiling water for 1–2 minutes. Drain and rinse under cold water, then squeeze the beans out of their skins.

Veal stroganoff

Preparation time 15 minutes • **Cooking time** 42 minutes • **Serves** 4

1 tablespoon vegetable oil
750 g (1 lb 10 oz) veal shin, cut into 5 cm
   (2 inch) chunks
160 g (5½ oz) bacon or speck, coarsely chopped
1 brown onion, finely chopped
2 tablespoons tomato paste (concentrated purée)

1 teaspoon smoked paprika
250 g (9 oz) button mushrooms, thickly sliced
1 red capsicum (pepper), cut into wide strips
1 tablespoon sour cream
finely snipped chives, to garnish
cooked fresh ribbon pasta, to serve

1 Heat the oil in a 6 litre (210 fl oz) pressure cooker over high heat and cook the veal in three batches for 4 minutes, or until well browned on all sides. Remove from the cooker and set aside.

2 Reduce the heat to medium. Add the bacon to the cooker and cook for 3 minutes, or until the bacon has browned and the fat has melted. Add the onion and cook for 3 minutes, stirring, until softened. Return the veal to the cooker with the tomato paste, paprika and 185 ml (6 fl oz/¾ cup) water. Season to taste with salt and freshly ground black pepper.

3 Lock the lid in place and bring the cooker to high pressure over medium–high heat. Once high pressure is reached, reduce the heat to stabilise the pressure and cook for 20 minutes, or until the veal is almost tender. Remove the cooker from the heat and release the pressure using the quick release method. Remove the lid carefully.

4 Stir in the mushrooms and capsicum. Lock the lid in place and bring the cooker to low pressure over high heat. Once low pressure is reached, reduce the heat to stabilise the pressure and cook for 4 minutes, or until the vegetables and veal are tender.

5 Remove the cooker from the heat and release the pressure using the natural release method. Remove the lid carefully. Stir in the sour cream.

6 Serve the stroganoff on a bed of pasta, sprinkled with chives.

NOTE: The stroganoff can be frozen in an airtight container for up to 3 months.

Osso buco bianco with potatoes and orange olive gremolata

Preparation time 40 minutes • **Cooking time** 41 minutes • **Serves** 4

8 (about 1.3 kg/3 lb) even-sized pieces of veal
   osso bucco, each about 4 cm (1½ inches) thick
1 tablespoon olive oil
20 g (¾ oz) butter
1 brown onion, finely chopped
2 garlic cloves, finely chopped
2 orange peel strips, each about 1 cm (½ inch)
   wide, white pith removed
250 ml (9 fl oz/1 cup) white wine
250 ml (9 fl oz/1 cup) good-quality purchased
   or homemade chicken stock (see page 14)
6 (about 350 g/12 oz) small new potatoes,
   peeled and halved

1 celery stalk, finely chopped
1 carrot, finely chopped

ORANGE OLIVE GREMOLATA
2 tablespoons finely chopped flat-leaf (Italian)
   parsley leaves
2 teaspoons finely grated orange zest
1 garlic clove, finely chopped
75 g (2½ oz/⅓ cup) pitted green olives,
   rinsed and very finely chopped

1 Pat the veal pieces dry with paper towels. Heat the oil in an 8 litre (280 fl oz) pressure cooker over high heat and cook the veal pieces in two batches, turning occasionally, for 4 minutes, or until browned. Remove from the cooker and set aside.

2 Melt the butter in the cooker over low heat and sauté the onion, garlic and orange peel strips for 5 minutes, or until soft but not browned. Increase the heat to high, stir in the wine and simmer for 2–3 minutes, or until reduced by half, scraping the base of the pot. Return the veal to the cooker with the stock and stir well.

3 Lock the lid in place and bring the cooker to high pressure over high heat. Once high pressure is reached, reduce the heat to stabilise the pressure and cook for 17 minutes, or until the veal is almost tender. Remove the cooker from the heat and release the pressure using the quick release method. Remove the lid carefully.

4 Add the potatoes, celery and carrot, replace the lid immediately and lock in place. Bring to high pressure over high heat. Once high pressure is reached, reduce the heat to stabilise the pressure and cook for 8 minutes, or until the potatoes and veal are tender. Remove the cooker from the heat and release the pressure using the natural release method. Remove the lid carefully. Remove and discard the orange peel strips.

5 To make the orange olive gremolata, combine all the ingredients in a small bowl and mix well.

6 Divide the veal and vegetables among warm plates. Stir half the gremolata through the sauce and spoon the sauce over the meat. Sprinkle with the remaining gremolata and serve.

Veal provençal

Preparation time 10 minutes • **Cooking time** 36 minutes • **Serves** 4

60 ml (2 fl oz/¼ cup) olive oil
1 large eggplant (aubergine), cut into 4 cm
  (1½ inch) chunks
700 g (1 lb 9 oz) veal shin, cut into 5 cm
  (2 inch) chunks
1 brown onion, diced

2 garlic cloves, thinly sliced
400 g (14 oz) tin chopped tomatoes
1 red capsicum (pepper), thickly sliced
60 g (2¼ oz/⅓ cup) black olives
mashed potato, to serve
finely shredded basil leaves, to garnish

1 Heat 1 tablespoon of the oil in an 8 litre
(280 fl oz) pressure cooker over medium–high heat
and cook the eggplant, stirring occasionally, for
5 minutes, or until browned and starting to soften.
Remove from the cooker and set aside.

2 Heat another 1 tablespoon of oil in the cooker
over high heat and cook the veal in two batches
for 2–3 minutes, or until well browned on all sides.
Remove from the cooker and set aside.

3 Heat the remaining oil in the cooker and cook
the onion for 3 minutes, stirring, until the onion
starts to soften. Stir in the garlic and cook until
aromatic. Return the veal to the cooker with the
tomatoes and 60 ml (2 fl oz/¼ cup) water. Season
to taste with salt and freshly ground black pepper
and stir well.

4 Lock the lid in place and bring the cooker to high
pressure over high heat. Once high pressure is
reached, reduce the heat to stabilise the pressure
and cook for 20 minutes, or until the veal is tender.

5 Remove the cooker from the heat and release
the pressure using the quick release method.
Remove the lid carefully, as the veal may spit
when moved.

6 Add the eggplant, capsicum and olives, replace
the lid immediately and lock in place. Bring the
cooker back to high pressure over high heat.
Once high pressure is reached, reduce the heat to
stabilise the pressure and cook for 2 minutes, or
until the vegetables are tender.

7 Remove the cooker from the heat and release
the pressure using the natural release method.
Remove the lid carefully.

8 Serve on a bed of mashed potato, garnished
with basil.

NOTE: This dish can be frozen in an airtight
container for up to 3 months.

PORK

Pork with apple and fennel

Preparation time 15 minutes • **Cooking time** 25 minutes • **Serves** 4–6

1 kg (2 lb 4 oz) boneless pork leg roast,
    trimmed and cut into 4 cm (1½ inch) chunks
1 tablespoon rosemary leaves
1 leek, pale section only, rinsed well, trimmed
    and chopped
1 apple (such as pink lady or fuji), peeled,
    cored and chopped
2 garlic cloves, finely chopped

250 ml (9 fl oz/1 cup) sparkling apple cider
1 small fennel bulb, trimmed and thickly sliced
100 g (3½ oz) button mushrooms, halved
500 g (1 lb 2 oz) sweet potato, peeled and
    cut into 3 cm (1¼ inch) chunks
2 tablespoons coarsely chopped flat-leaf
    (Italian) parsley leaves
steamed English spinach, to serve

1 Place the pork in a 6 litre (210 fl oz) pressure cooker. Sprinkle with the rosemary, season well with salt and freshly ground black pepper and gently toss to coat.

2 Add the leek, apple, garlic and cider to the cooker and gently mix to combine. Lock the lid in place and bring the cooker to high pressure over high heat. Once high pressure is reached, reduce the heat to stabilise the pressure and cook for 20 minutes, or until the pork is almost tender.

3 Remove the cooker from the heat and release the pressure using the quick release method. Remove the lid carefully.

4 Add the fennel, mushrooms and sweet potato, replace the lid immediately and lock in place. Bring the cooker to low pressure over high heat. Once low pressure is reached, reduce the heat to stabilise the pressure and cook for 5 minutes, or until the sweet potato is tender.

5 Remove the cooker from the heat and release the pressure using the natural release method. Remove the lid carefully.

6 Serve the pork mixture sprinkled with the parsley and freshly ground black pepper, with steamed spinach on the side.

Pork ribs with corn salsa

Preparation time 15 minutes • **Cooking time** 25 minutes • **Serves** 4

1.25 kg (2 lb 12 oz) pork barbecue ribs (rib racks, not pork belly ribs)
1 red onion, finely chopped
1 green capsicum (pepper), finely chopped
1 green chilli, seeded and finely chopped
2 garlic cloves, finely chopped
185 ml (6 fl oz/¾ cup) barbecue sauce
2 tablespoons white wine vinegar
1 tablespoon sweet chilli sauce
2 teaspoons worcestershire sauce
a dash of Tabasco sauce

coriander (cilantro) leaves, to garnish (optional)
cherry tomatoes, to serve

CORN SALSA
350 g (12 oz) fresh or frozen corn kernels (about 1¾ cups fresh kernels, or 2⅓ cups frozen)
2 spring onions (scallions), finely chopped
1 tablespoon finely chopped coriander (cilantro) leaves
1 tablespoon extra virgin olive oil
2 tablespoons lime juice

1 Cut the ribs into sets of two or three and trim off any excess fat. Place the ribs in an 8 litre (280 fl oz) pressure cooker with the onion, capsicum, chilli, garlic, barbecue sauce, vinegar, sweet chilli sauce, worcestershire sauce, Tabasco and 185 ml (6 fl oz/ ¾ cup) water. Season to taste with salt and freshly ground black pepper and stir to combine.

2 Lock the lid in place and bring the cooker to high pressure over high heat. Once high pressure is reached, reduce the heat to stabilise the pressure and cook for 15 minutes, or until the ribs are tender.

3 Meanwhile, to make the corn salsa, bring a saucepan of water to the boil over high heat. Add the corn and cook for 2–3 minutes, or until just tender. Rinse under cold running water to cool. Drain well, then place in a bowl. Add the spring onion, coriander, oil and lime juice and gently toss to combine. Season to taste.

4 Remove the cooker from the heat and release the pressure using the natural release method. Remove the lid carefully.

5 Using a slotted spoon, transfer the ribs and vegetables to a warmed plate and cover to keep warm, leaving the liquid in the cooker. Place the cooker over high heat and boil, uncovered and stirring regularly, for 5–10 minutes, or until the sauce is reduced to a glaze consistency. Turn off the heat, return the ribs and vegetables to the cooker and stir gently to coat in the sauce.

6 Serve the ribs garnished with coriander, if desired, and accompanied by cherry tomatoes and the corn salsa.

Mojo pork

Preparation time 25 minutes • **Cooking time** 25 minutes • **Serves** 6

1.5 kg (3 lb 5 oz) pork scotch (pork neck),
   trimmed and cut into 3 cm (1¼ inch) chunks
2 tablespoons olive oil
2 teaspoons dried oregano
1 teaspoon chilli flakes
½ teaspoon freshly ground black pepper
1 large red onion, thinly sliced
2 x 400 g (14 oz) tins chopped tomatoes
60 ml (2 fl oz/¼ cup) lime juice
60 ml (2 fl oz/¼ cup) orange juice
80 ml (2½ fl oz/⅓ cup) good-quality purchased
   or homemade chicken stock (see page 14)
coriander (cilantro) leaves, to garnish

BEAN AND ORANGE SALAD
2 oranges, peel and white pith removed,
   cut into segments
400 g (14 oz) tin butterbeans (lima beans),
   rinsed and drained
400 g (14 oz) tin chickpeas, rinsed and drained
½ small red onion, thinly sliced
⅓ cup coriander (cilantro) leaves
1 tablespoon olive oil
1 tablespoon red wine vinegar
a pinch of sugar

1 Place all the mojo pork ingredients except the coriander in a 6 litre (210 fl oz) pressure cooker. Mix to combine evenly.

2 Lock the lid in place and bring the cooker to high pressure over high heat. Once high pressure is reached, reduce the heat to stabilise the pressure and cook for 25 minutes, or until the pork is tender.

3 Meanwhile, to make the bean and orange salad, combine the orange segments, beans, chickpeas, onion and coriander. Whisk together the oil, vinegar and sugar until the sugar has dissolved. Season to taste with salt and freshly ground black pepper, drizzle over the salad and gently toss.

4 Remove the cooker from the heat and release the pressure using the natural release method. Remove the lid carefully.

5 Ladle the pork mixture onto serving plates. Garnish with coriander and serve with the bean and orange salad.

NOTE: 'Mojo' refers to a sauce that contains spices and citrus juice (generally lime and/or orange juice). Mojo sauce is used in Cuban cooking.

Pork and bean stew

Preparation time 10 minutes • **Cooking time** 35 minutes • **Serves** 4

2 tablespoons olive oil
750 g (1 lb 10 oz) pork shoulder, trimmed
   and cut into 5 cm (2 inch) chunks
1 brown onion, finely chopped
3 garlic cloves, crushed
1 tablespoon rosemary leaves

400 g (14 oz) tin chopped tomatoes
2 x 400 g (14 oz) tins cannellini beans, rinsed
   and drained, then roughly chopped
chopped flat-leaf (Italian) parsley leaves,
   to garnish

1 Heat the oil in a 6 litre (210 fl oz) pressure cooker over medium–high heat and cook the pork in three batches for 4 minutes, or until well browned on all sides. Remove from the cooker and set aside.

2 Reduce the heat to medium. Add the onion, garlic and rosemary to the cooker and cook for 3 minutes, stirring, until softened. Return the pork to the cooker with the tomatoes. Season to taste with salt and freshly ground black pepper.

3 Lock the lid in place and bring the cooker to high pressure over medium–high heat. Once high pressure is reached, reduce the heat to stabilise the pressure and cook for 15 minutes. Remove the cooker from the heat and release the pressure using the quick release method. Remove the lid carefully.

4 Stir in the beans. Lock the lid in place and bring the cooker to high pressure over high heat. Once high pressure is reached, reduce the heat to stabilise the pressure and cook for 5 minutes.

5 Remove the cooker from the heat and release the pressure using the natural release method. Remove the lid carefully.

6 Serve the stew garnished with parsley.

NOTE: This dish can be frozen in an airtight container for up to 3 months.

Cameroon pork curry

Preparation time 30 minutes • **Cooking time** 35 minutes • **Serves** 4–6

40 g (1½ oz) butter

1 brown onion, chopped

3 garlic cloves, crushed

2 tablespoons mild Indian curry powder

1 teaspoon chilli flakes

1.25 kg (2 lb 12 oz) boneless pork leg, trimmed and cut into 2.5 cm (1 inch) chunks

310 ml (10¾ fl oz/1¼ cups) good-quality purchased or homemade chicken stock (see page 14)

125 ml (4 fl oz/½ cup) coconut cream

1 (about 200 g/7 oz) sweet potato, peeled and cut into 2 cm (¾ inch) chunks

1 green capsicum (pepper), cut into 2 cm (¾ inch) pieces

½ small ripe, sweet pineapple, trimmed, cored and cut into 2 cm (¾ inch) chunks

35 g (1¼ oz/½ cup) shredded coconut

1 banana, peeled and sliced

1 mango, peeled and cubed (see Note)

45 g (1¼ oz/¼ cup) roasted peanuts, chopped

naan bread, to serve

lime wedges, to serve

1 Melt the butter in an 8 litre (280 fl oz) pressure cooker over medium–high heat and cook the onion for 5 minutes, or until softened. Add the garlic, curry powder and chilli flakes and cook, stirring often, for 1 minute, or until aromatic. Add the pork and toss well to coat in the spices. Stir in the stock and half the coconut cream.

2 Lock the lid in place and bring the cooker to high pressure over high heat. Once high pressure is reached, reduce the heat to stabilise the pressure and cook for 22 minutes, or until the pork is almost tender. Remove the cooker from the heat and release the pressure using the quick release method. Remove the lid carefully.

3 Add the sweet potato, capsicum and pineapple, replace the lid immediately and lock in place. Bring the cooker back to high pressure over high heat. Once high pressure is reached, reduce the heat to stabilise the pressure and cook for 4 minutes, or until the pork and vegetables are tender.

4 Remove the cooker from the heat and release the pressure using the natural release method. Remove the lid carefully. Stir in the remaining coconut cream and simmer for 2–3 minutes, or until the sauce is slightly thickened.

5 Meanwhile, place the shredded coconut in a small bowl and roll the banana in the coconut to coat. Place the mango and peanuts in separate small bowls to serve as garnishes for the curry.

6 Serve the curry with the banana, mango, peanuts, naan bread and lime wedges.

NOTE: If mangoes are not in season, use a drained 400 g (14 oz) tin of mango pieces instead.

Thai chilli pork spare ribs

Preparation time 10 minutes • **Cooking time** 15–25 minutes • **Serves** 4

250 ml (9 fl oz/1 cup) Thai sweet chilli sauce
2 tablespoons tomato sauce (ketchup)
2 tablespoons dry sherry
2 tablespoons fish sauce
2 garlic cloves, crushed
1 tablespoon finely grated fresh ginger
1.5 kg (3 lb 5 oz) American-style pork spare ribs
cooked jasmine rice (see page 12), to serve
lime wedges, to serve (optional)

APPLE SALAD
1 green apple, cored and cut into thick
  matchsticks
1/3 cup coriander (cilantro) leaves
1 green chilli, seeded and thinly sliced
  (optional)
1 tablespoon lime juice
a pinch of salt

1 Combine the chilli sauce, tomato sauce, sherry, fish sauce, garlic, ginger and 375 ml (13 fl oz/1½ cups) water in a 6 litre (210 fl oz) pressure cooker and stir to combine. Cut the ribs into segments of three ribs each. Add the ribs to the cooker and gently stir.

2 Lock the lid in place and bring the cooker to high pressure over high heat. Once high pressure is reached, reduce the heat to stabilise the pressure and cook for 15 minutes, or until the ribs are tender.

3 Meanwhile, to make the apple salad, combine all the ingredients in a bowl and mix gently. Cover and refrigerate until required.

4 Remove the cooker from the heat and release the pressure using the natural release method. Remove the lid carefully.

5 If the sauce needs thickening, use a slotted spoon to transfer the ribs to a warm plate; cover with foil to keep warm. Place the cooker back over high heat and boil, uncovered, for 10 minutes, or until the sauce has reduced to a glaze.

6 Divide the ribs among serving plates and drizzle with the sauce. Serve with the apple salad and lime wedges, if desired.

LAMB

Greek lamb with risoni and feta

Preparation time 20 minutes • **Cooking time** 20 minutes • **Serves** 4

1.25 kg (2 lb 12 oz) boneless lamb leg,
   trimmed and cut into 4 cm (1½ inch) chunks
2 small red onions, finely chopped
2 garlic cloves, crushed
2 bay leaves
2 x 400 g (14 oz) tins chopped tomatoes
80 ml (2½ fl oz/⅓ cup) good-quality purchased
   or homemade chicken stock (see page 14)

80 ml (2½ fl oz/⅓ cup) white wine
220 g (7¾ oz/1 cup) risoni (see Note)
75 g (2½ oz/½ cup) crumbled feta cheese
finely grated zest of 1 lemon
2 tablespoons small oregano leaves
Greek salad, to serve
crusty bread, to serve (optional)

1 Place the lamb, onion, garlic, bay leaves, tomatoes and a pinch of salt in a 6 litre (210 fl oz) pressure cooker. Add the stock and wine and stir to combine.

2 Lock the lid in place and bring the cooker to high pressure over high heat. Once high pressure is reached, reduce the heat to stabilise the pressure and cook for 20 minutes, or until the lamb is very tender.

3 Meanwhile, cook the risoni in a large saucepan of salted boiling water following packet directions until al dente. Drain and rinse.

4 Remove the cooker from the heat and release the pressure using the natural release method. Remove the lid carefully.

5 Gently stir the drained risoni through the lamb mixture and season well with salt and freshly ground black pepper.

6 Serve sprinkled with the feta, lemon zest and oregano leaves, with a Greek salad and crusty bread on the side, if desired.

NOTE: Risoni, also known as orzo, is a small rice-shaped pasta. You'll find it in the pasta section of supermarkets. If it is unavailable, use another small pasta shape instead.

Lamb shanks with quince paste

Preparation time 10 minutes • **Cooking time** 47 minutes • **Serves** 6

35 g (1¼ oz/¼ cup) plain (all-purpose) flour
6 large (about 2 kg/4 lb 8 oz) French-trimmed
  lamb shanks
60 ml (2 fl oz/¼ cup) olive oil
80 ml (2½ fl oz/⅓ cup) red wine vinegar
1 brown onion, chopped
2 garlic cloves, finely chopped
95 g (3¼ oz/½ cup) dried Turkish apricots
½ teaspoon sweet paprika
½ teaspoon ground turmeric
½ teaspoon ground allspice

¼ teaspoon ground cardamom
375 ml (13 fl oz/1½ cups) good-quality purchased
  or homemade chicken stock (see page 14)
2 (about 400 g/14 oz) all-purpose potatoes,
  peeled and cut into 1.5 cm (⅝ inch) chunks
1 carrot, thinly sliced on the diagonal
160 g (5½ oz/1 cup) pitted dates, chopped
100 g (3½ oz) quince paste, cut into small
  pieces (see Note)
mashed potato, to serve
flaked almonds, toasted, to serve

1 Season the flour with salt and freshly ground black pepper. Dust the lamb shanks in the flour, shaking off the excess.

2 Heat the oil in an 8 litre (280 fl oz) pressure cooker over medium–high heat and cook the shanks in two batches for 8 minutes, or until well browned on all sides, turning occasionally. Remove from the cooker and set aside. Discard the excess oil from the cooker.

3 Add the vinegar to the cooker and simmer for 2 minutes, or until reduced by half, scraping the base of the pot. Return the shanks to the cooker with the onion, garlic, apricots, spices and stock. Stir to combine.

4 Lock the lid in place and bring the cooker to high pressure over high heat. Once high pressure is reached, reduce the heat to stabilise the pressure and cook for 20 minutes, or until the lamb is almost tender. Remove the cooker from the heat and release the pressure using the quick release method. Remove the lid carefully.

5 Add the potato and carrot to the cooker, replace the lid immediately and lock in place. Bring the cooker back to high pressure over high heat. Once high pressure is reached, reduce the heat to stabilise the pressure and cook for 6 minutes, or until the lamb and vegetables are tender.

6 Remove the cooker from the heat and release the pressure using the natural release method. Remove the lid carefully. Remove the shanks to a warm plate and cover with foil to keep warm. Add the dates and quince paste to the cooker and simmer for 2–3 minutes, or until the quince paste is incorporated and the dates are warmed through.

7 Serve on a bed of mashed potato, sprinkled with flaked almonds.

NOTE: Quince paste is available from the cheese or deli section of larger supermarkets.

Lebanese lamb stew

Preparation time 20 minutes • **Cooking time** 21 minutes • **Serves** 4–6

1 kg (2 lb 4 oz) boneless lamb shoulder,
  trimmed and cut into 3 cm (1¼ inch) chunks
2 teaspoons sumac (see Note)
1 teaspoon mixed (pumpkin pie) spice
½ teaspoon freshly ground black pepper
1 brown onion, finely chopped
3 garlic cloves, crushed
2 tablespoons tomato paste (concentrated purée)
125 ml (4 fl oz/½ cup) tomato passata
  (puréed tomatoes)

185 ml (6 fl oz/¾ cup) good-quality purchased
  or homemade chicken stock (see page 14)
400 g (14 oz) tin cannellini beans, rinsed
  and drained
coriander (cilantro) leaves, to garnish
lemon cheeks, to serve
green salad, to serve

1 Place the lamb, sumac, mixed spice and pepper in a mixing bowl. Season with salt and toss well to combine. Transfer the lamb to a 6 litre (210 fl oz) pressure cooker. Add the onion, garlic, tomato paste, passata and stock and stir to combine.

2 Lock the lid in place and bring the cooker to high pressure over high heat. Once high pressure is reached, reduce the heat to stabilise the pressure and cook for 20 minutes, or until the lamb is very tender. Remove the cooker from the heat and release the pressure using the natural release method. Remove the lid carefully.

3 Stir in the beans, season to taste with salt and freshly ground black pepper and simmer, uncovered, for 1 minute, or until the beans are heated through.

4 Divide the lamb among serving bowls and garnish with coriander. Serve with the lemon cheeks and a green salad.

NOTE: Sumac is a ground spice from the sumac berry, which grows throughout the Middle East. It has a purplish-red colour and slightly lemony taste. You'll find it in selected delicatessens, spice shops and gourmet food stores.

Chilli and anchovy lamb neck

Preparation time 25 minutes • **Cooking time** 10 minutes • **Serves** 6

4 drained anchovy fillets, finely chopped
2 garlic cloves, finely chopped
1 large red chilli, finely chopped
1.5 kg (3 lb 5 oz) lamb neck chops, trimmed
  of excess fat and sinew
1 brown onion, finely chopped
1 celery stalk, finely chopped
1 carrot, finely chopped
400 g (14 oz) tin chopped tomatoes

60 ml (2 fl oz/¼ cup) good-quality purchased
  or homemade chicken stock (see page 14)
125 ml (4 fl oz/½ cup) red wine
1 cup finely chopped flat-leaf (Italian) parsley
  leaves
finely grated zest of ½ orange
mashed potato, to serve
steamed green beans, to serve

1 Mix together the anchovy, garlic and chilli in a small bowl. Spread the mixture over both sides of the lamb chops, then season well with freshly ground black pepper. Combine the onion, celery and carrot in a bowl, then place with the chops in alternating layers in an 8 litre (280 fl oz) pressure cooker. Combine the tomatoes, stock, wine and half the parsley and add to the cooker.

2 Lock the lid in place and bring the cooker to high pressure over high heat. Once high pressure is reached, reduce the heat to stabilise the pressure and cook for 10 minutes, or until the lamb is tender.

3 Meanwhile, combine the remaining parsley and the orange zest in a small bowl.

4 Remove the cooker from the heat and release the pressure using the natural release method. Remove the lid carefully.

5 Divide the lamb among serving plates and drizzle with the sauce. Sprinkle with the parsley and orange zest mixture and serve with mashed potato and steamed green beans.

Lamb shanks with lentils

Preparation time 25 minutes • **Cooking time** 28 minutes • **Serves** 4

1 brown onion, chopped
1 carrot, chopped
1 celery stalk, chopped
1 parsnip, peeled and chopped
50 g (1¾ oz) thickly sliced pancetta or bacon, chopped
2 garlic cloves, chopped
2 drained anchovy fillets, finely chopped
4 (about 1.4 kg/3 lb 2 oz) French-trimmed lamb shanks

125 ml (4 fl oz/½ cup) good-quality purchased or homemade chicken stock (see page 14)
125 ml (4 fl oz/½ cup) red wine
1 tablespoon olive oil
100 g (3½ oz) button mushrooms, halved
400 g (14 oz) tin brown lentils, rinsed and drained
chopped flat-leaf (Italian) parsley leaves, to garnish
purchased horseradish cream, to serve

1 Combine the onion, carrot, celery, parsnip, pancetta, garlic and anchovies in an 8 litre (280 fl oz) pressure cooker and spread over the base. Arrange the shanks over the mixture, then season with salt and freshly ground black pepper. Pour the stock and wine over the shanks.

2 Lock the lid in place and bring the cooker to high pressure over high heat. Once high pressure is reached, reduce the heat to stabilise the pressure and cook for 25 minutes, or until the lamb is tender. Remove the cooker from the heat and release the pressure using the natural release method. Remove the lid carefully.

3 Meanwhile, heat the oil in a frying pan over medium–high heat and cook the mushrooms for 3–4 minutes, or until tender and golden.

4 Add the mushrooms and lentils to the shanks and season to taste. Place the cooker back over medium heat and simmer, uncovered, for 2–3 minutes, or until the lentils and mushrooms are heated through.

5 Serve sprinkled with parsley, and with a small bowl of horseradish cream on the side.

Curried lamb and rice meatballs

Preparation time 20 minutes (+ 5 minutes standing) • **Cooking time** 7 minutes • **Serves** 4

500 g (1 lb 2 oz) minced (ground) lamb
100 g (3½ oz/½ cup) jasmine rice
55 g (2 oz/½ cup) dry breadcrumbs
1 egg
2 tablespoons finely chopped coriander
  (cilantro) leaves
1 tablespoon peanut oil
55 g (2 oz/¼ cup) purchased panang curry paste
400 ml (14 fl oz) tin coconut milk, plus a 270 ml
  (9½ fl oz) tin

300 g (10½ oz) sweet potato, peeled, halved
  lengthways and thickly sliced
300 g (10½ oz) green beans, trimmed and
  halved
3 carrots, cut into 4 cm (1½ inch) chunks,
  then thickly sliced lengthways
2 tablespoons fish sauce
small basil leaves, to garnish
lime wedges, to serve

1 Place the lamb, rice, breadcrumbs, egg and coriander in a bowl and mix well until evenly combined. Roll heaped tablespoons of the mixture into balls.

2 Heat the oil in a 6 litre (210 fl oz) pressure cooker over medium–high heat and cook the curry paste for 30 seconds, or until aromatic. Stir in 500 ml (17 fl oz/2 cups) of the coconut milk. Add the meatballs and gently stir to cover with the sauce. Without stirring, add the sweet potato, then the beans and finally the carrot.

3 Lock the lid in place and bring the cooker to low pressure over medium–high heat. Once low pressure is reached, reduce the heat to stabilise the pressure and cook for 5 minutes.

4 Remove the cooker from the heat and release the pressure using the natural release method. Remove the lid carefully.

5 Gently stir the remaining coconut milk and fish sauce through. Cover and set aside for 5 minutes (the sauce will thicken on standing).

6 Serve sprinkled with basil leaves, accompanied by lime wedges.

NOTE: It is important that you don't stir the vegetables into the sauce when you add them to the cooker. This way they will be 'steamed' rather than stewed, and will be less likely to become overcooked and fall apart.

Moroccan honey lamb shanks with root vegetables

Preparation time 30 minutes • **Cooking time** 48 minutes • **Serves** 4

1 tablespoon olive oil
4 (about 1.25 kg/2 lb 12 oz) French-trimmed
  lamb shanks
1 brown onion, halved and sliced
2 garlic cloves, crushed
2 tablespoons Moroccan spice mix
435 ml (15¼ fl oz/1¾ cups) good-quality
  purchased or homemade chicken stock
  (see page 14)
90 g (3¼ oz/¼ cup) honey

1 parsnip
1 large carrot
300 g (10½ oz) sweet potato
60 g (2¼ oz/⅓ cup) raisins
2 lemon peel strips, each about 2 cm (¾ inch)
  wide, white pith removed (see Note)
140 g (5 oz/1 cup) frozen peas
slivered almonds, toasted, to garnish
chopped flat-leaf (Italian) parsley leaves,
  to garnish

1 Heat the oil in an 8 litre (280 fl oz) pressure cooker over high heat and cook the shanks in two batches for 8 minutes, or until well browned on all sides. Remove from the cooker and set aside.

2 Reduce the heat to medium. Add the onion and garlic to the cooker and cook for 5 minutes, or until the onion has softened. Stir in the Moroccan spice mix and cook for 1 minute, or until aromatic. Stir in the stock and honey and combine well.

3 Lock the lid in place and bring the cooker to high pressure over high heat. Once high pressure is reached, reduce the heat to stabilise the pressure and cook for 20 minutes, or until the lamb is almost tender.

4 Meanwhile, peel the parsnip, carrot and sweet potato and cut into 4 cm (1½ inch) chunks.

5 Remove the cooker from the heat and release the pressure using the quick release method. Remove the lid carefully. Add the parsnip, carrot, sweet potato, raisins and lemon peel strips to the cooker and stir briefly to combine. Replace the lid

immediately and lock in place. Bring the cooker back to high pressure over high heat. Once high pressure is reached, reduce the heat to stabilise the pressure and cook for 5 minutes, or until the lamb and vegetables are tender.

6 Remove the cooker from the heat and release the pressure using the natural release method. Remove the lid carefully. Remove the lemon peel strips.

7 Stir in the peas, season to taste with salt and freshly ground black pepper and cook, uncovered, over medium heat for 1 minute, or until the peas are warmed through. (If the sauce is not as thick as you would like, remove the shanks and vegetables and boil the sauce a little longer until reduced to the desired consistency.)

8 Divide the shanks among warm serving plates. Spoon the sauce and vegetables over the shanks, garnish with almonds and parsley and serve.

NOTE: Instead of lemon peel strips, you can add the rinsed and thinly sliced rind of a quarter of a preserved lemon.

Navarin of lamb

Preparation time 20 minutes • **Cooking time** 45 minutes • **Serves** 6

35 g (1¼ oz/¼ cup) plain (all-purpose) flour
6 large (about 2 kg/4 lb 8 oz each) French-
   trimmed lamb shanks
2 tablespoons olive oil
1 brown onion, finely chopped
2 garlic cloves, crushed
250 ml (9 fl oz/1 cup) white wine
250 ml (9 fl oz/1 cup) good-quality purchased
   or homemade chicken stock (see page 14)

2 tablespoons tomato paste (concentrated purée)
12 small new potatoes
3 small turnips, peeled and cut into 3 cm
   (1¼ inch) wedges
12 small pickling onions, trimmed and peeled
1 rosemary sprig
110 g (3¾ oz/¾ cup) frozen green peas
mashed potato, to serve
steamed baby carrots, to serve

1 Season 2 tablespoons of the flour with salt and freshly ground black pepper. Toss the lamb shanks in the seasoned flour until well coated, then shake off the excess flour.

2 Heat the oil in an 8 litre (280 fl oz) pressure cooker over medium–high heat and cook half the shanks for 8 minutes, turning to brown all over. Remove from the cooker and set aside. Repeat with the remaining shanks.

3 Add the onion, garlic, wine, stock and tomato paste to the cooker and simmer for 2 minutes, scraping the base of the pot. Return the shanks to the cooker and stir well.

4 Lock the lid in place and bring the cooker to high pressure over high heat. Once high pressure is reached, reduce the heat to stabilise the pressure and cook for 20 minutes, or until the lamb is almost tender. Remove the cooker from the heat and release the pressure using the quick release method. Remove the lid carefully.

5 Add the potatoes, turnip, pickling onions and rosemary, replace the lid immediately and lock in place. Bring the cooker back to high pressure over high heat. Once high pressure is reached, reduce the heat to stabilise the pressure and cook for 6 minutes, or until the vegetables are almost tender. Remove the cooker from the heat and release the pressure using the natural release method. Remove the lid carefully.

6 Skim off any fat from the surface of the sauce. Stir in the peas and place the cooker over medium–high heat. Simmer, uncovered, for 1 minute, or until the peas are warmed through. Season to taste.

7 Serve the lamb and vegetables with mashed potato, with steamed baby carrots on the side.

Lamb rogan josh

Preparation time 15 minutes • **Cooking time** 32 minutes • **Serves** 4

6 (about 1 kg/2 lb 4 oz) lamb forequarter chops
2 tablespoons ghee (see Notes)
2 brown onions, thinly sliced
1 tablespoon finely grated fresh ginger
2 tablespoons rogan josh curry paste
half a 400 g (14 oz) tin chopped tomatoes

2 tablespoons chopped coriander
   (cilantro) leaves
2 tablespoons chopped mint leaves
1 fresh long green chilli, finely chopped
cooked basmati rice (see page 12), to serve
2 tablespoons slivered almonds, toasted

1 Remove the fat and bones from the lamb chops, then cut the meat into 4 cm (1½ inch) chunks.

2 Heat half the ghee in a 6 litre (210 fl oz) pressure cooker over medium–high heat and cook the lamb in two batches for 3 minutes, or until well browned. Remove from the cooker and set aside.

3 Heat the remaining ghee in the cooker over medium–high heat and cook the onion for 7 minutes, or until well browned, stirring occasionally. Stir in the ginger and curry paste and cook for 1 minute, or until the mixture is aromatic. Add the tomatoes and 80 ml (2½ fl oz/⅓ cup) water. Return the lamb to the cooker.

4 Lock the lid in place and bring the cooker to high pressure over medium–high heat. Once high pressure is reached, reduce the heat to stabilise the pressure and cook for 18 minutes, or until the lamb is very tender.

5 Meanwhile, combine the coriander, mint and chilli in a small bowl.

6 Remove the cooker from the heat and release the pressure using the natural release method. Remove the lid carefully.

7 Serve the curry on a bed of rice, garnished with the coriander mixture and the almonds.

NOTES: Ghee is clarified butter. Because the milk solids have been removed, it can be heated to a high temperature without burning. You will find ghee in the dairy section of supermarkets.
   This dish can be frozen in an airtight container for up to 3 months.

VEGETARIAN

Indian-style vegetable curry

Preparation time 20 minutes • **Cooking time** 6 minutes • **Serves** 4

300 g (10½ oz) sweet potato, peeled and
   cut into 2 cm (¾ inch) chunks
1 brown onion, finely chopped
2 teaspoons finely grated fresh ginger
55 g (2 oz/¼ cup) mild curry paste (such as balti)
2 tablespoons curry leaves (see Note)
375 ml (13 fl oz/1½ cups) good-quality purchased
   or homemade vegetable stock (see page 18)
375 g (13 oz/3 cups) large cauliflower florets

1 zucchini (courgette), quartered lengthways
   and cut into 3 cm (1¼ inch) thick lengths
2 ripe tomatoes, chopped
400 g (14 oz) tin brown lentils, rinsed and drained
100 g (3½ oz) baby spinach leaves
140 g (5 oz/1 cup) frozen peas
¼ cup chopped coriander (cilantro) leaves
70 g (2½ oz/¼ cup) plain yoghurt
cooked basmati rice (see page 12), to serve

1 Place the sweet potato, onion, ginger, curry paste, curry leaves and stock in a 6 litre (210 fl oz) pressure cooker and mix to combine. Season to taste with salt and freshly ground black pepper.

2 Lock the lid in place and bring the cooker to low pressure over high heat. Once low pressure is reached, reduce the heat to stabilise the pressure and cook for 2 minutes. Remove the cooker from the heat and release the pressure using the quick release method. Remove the lid carefully.

3 Add the cauliflower, zucchini and tomato, replace the lid immediately and lock in place. Bring the cooker back to low pressure over high heat. Once low pressure is reached, reduce the heat to stabilise the pressure and cook for 3 minutes, or until the vegetables are tender. Remove the cooker from the heat and release the pressure using the quick release method. Remove the lid carefully.

4 Stir in the lentils, spinach, peas and half the coriander. Place the cooker over medium heat and cook, uncovered, stirring regularly, for 1 minute, or until the peas are warmed through and the spinach has wilted. Remove from the heat and stir the yoghurt through.

5 Serve the curry with rice, sprinkled with the remaining coriander.

NOTE: Curry leaves are highly aromatic and used extensively in Sri Lankan and southern Indian cooking, particularly in curries. They are available from larger supermarkets, selected fruit and vegetable stores and Asian grocers.

Moroccan ratatouille with chickpeas

Preparation time 20 minutes • **Cooking time** 16 minutes • **Serves** 6

80 ml (2½ fl oz/⅓ cup) olive oil
2 (about 450 g/1 lb each) eggplants (aubergines),
    trimmed and cut into 2.5 cm (1 inch) chunks
2 large red onions, cut into 2 cm (¾ inch) chunks
2 large red capsicums (peppers), cut into
    2.5 cm (1 inch) chunks
2 tablespoons Moroccan spice mix (see Notes)
250 ml (9 fl oz/1 cup) good-quality purchased
    or homemade vegetable stock (see page 18)
2 tablespoons tomato paste (concentrated purée)
400 g (14 oz) tin chickpeas, rinsed and drained
750 g (1 lb 10 oz) butternut pumpkin (squash),
    peeled, seeded and cut into 3 cm (1¼ inch)
    chunks

2 x 400 g (14 oz) tins chopped tomatoes
260 g (9¼ oz/1 cup) Greek-style yoghurt
1 tablespoon finely chopped mint leaves
2 tablespoons lemon juice
3 teaspoons honey
120 g (4¼ oz/⅔ cup) pimento-stuffed
    green olives
2 tablespoons chopped coriander (cilantro)
    leaves
cooked white long-grain rice (see page 12),
    to serve
harissa, to serve (see Notes)

1 Heat 1½ tablespoons of the oil in an 8 litre (280 fl oz) pressure cooker over medium–high heat. Cook the eggplant in two batches for 4 minutes, tossing occasionally, until the eggplant has softened slightly and is light golden, adding more oil as necessary. Remove from the cooker and set aside.

2 Heat another tablespoon of oil in the cooker over medium–high heat and cook the onion for 3 minutes, or until it starts to soften. Add the capsicum and Moroccan spice mix and cook for 1 minute. Add the stock and tomato paste and simmer for 1 minute, scraping the base of the pot. Without stirring, add the eggplant, chickpeas and pumpkin in separate layers. Pour the tomatoes over the pumpkin (do not stir).

3 Lock the lid in place and bring the cooker to low pressure over medium–high heat. Once low pressure is reached, reduce the heat to stabilise the pressure and cook for 3 minutes, or until the vegetables are tender.

4 Meanwhile, mix together the yoghurt and mint.

5 Remove the cooker from the heat and release the pressure using the natural release method. Remove the lid carefully.

6 Gently stir in the lemon juice, honey, olives and coriander. Season to taste with salt and freshly ground black pepper.

7 Serve the ratatouille on a bed of rice, with the minted yoghurt and harissa.

NOTES: You'll find Moroccan spice mix in the spice aisle of your supermarket.
    Harissa is a hot, chilli-based sauce or paste widely used in North African cuisine. It is available from larger supermarkets, selected delicatessens and gourmet food stores.

Easy vegetarian chilli

Preparation time 15 minutes • **Cooking time** 13 minutes • **Serves** 4

2 tablespoons olive oil
1 large brown onion, finely diced
3 garlic cloves, crushed
½ teaspoon dried oregano
½ teaspoon dried thyme
1 tablespoon tomato paste (concentrated purée)
1 teaspoon ground cumin
1 red capsicum (pepper), cut into 2 cm
   (¾ inch) chunks
1 green capsicum (pepper), cut into 2 cm
   (¾ inch) chunks

185 ml (6 fl oz/¾ cup) good-quality purchased
   or homemade vegetable stock (see page 18)
½ teaspoon chilli flakes
2 bay leaves
2 x 400 g (14 oz) tins four-bean mix, rinsed
   and drained
310 g (11 oz) tin corn kernels
400 g (14 oz) tin chopped tomatoes
1 cup chopped coriander (cilantro) leaves
grated cheddar cheese, to serve (optional)
crusty bread, to serve

1 Heat the oil in a 6 litre (210 fl oz) pressure cooker over medium heat and cook the onion, garlic, oregano and thyme for 3 minutes, or until the onion is softened and translucent. Add the tomato paste, cumin and all the capsicum and stir to coat the capsicum in the tomato paste.

2 Pour in the stock and stir well. Add the chilli flakes, bay leaves, beans, corn and tomatoes and season to taste with salt and freshly ground black pepper.

3 Lock the lid in place and bring the cooker to high pressure over high heat. Once high pressure is reached, reduce the heat to stabilise the pressure

and cook for 5 minutes. Remove the cooker from the heat and release the pressure using the quick release method. Remove the lid carefully.

4 Place the cooker over medium heat and simmer, uncovered, for 5 minutes, or until the sauce has thickened. Stir the coriander through.

5 Serve sprinkled with cheese if desired, with crusty bread on the side.

Vegetable curry

Preparation time 15 minutes • **Cooking time** 9 minutes • **Serves** 4

1 tablespoon peanut oil

1 large red onion, cut into 1 cm (½ inch) wedges

55 g (2 oz/¼ cup) Malaysian curry paste

125 ml (4 fl oz/½ cup) good-quality purchased or homemade vegetable stock (see page 18)

2 teaspoons tamarind purée (see Note)

1 teaspoon chilli powder, or to taste

1 teaspoon grated palm sugar (jaggery) or brown sugar

270 ml (9½ fl oz) tin coconut milk

300 g (10½ oz) all-purpose potatoes, peeled and cut into 2 cm (¾ inch) dice

300 g (10½ oz) pumpkin (winter squash), peeled, seeded and cut into 4 cm (1½ inch) chunks

300 g (10½ oz) green beans, trimmed and halved

425 g (15 oz) tin whole baby corn, drained and cut into 3 cm (1¼ inch) pieces

cooked jasmine rice (see page 12), to serve

coriander (cilantro) leaves, to garnish

1 Heat the oil in an 8 litre (280 fl oz) pressure cooker over medium heat and cook the onion with a pinch of salt for 3 minutes, or until softened. Add the curry paste and cook, stirring, for 30 seconds, or until aromatic.

2 Add the stock, tamarind purée, chilli powder, palm sugar and 125 ml (4 fl oz/½ cup) of the coconut milk and stir well. Add all the vegetables and stir to combine.

3 Lock the lid in place and bring the cooker to low pressure over high heat. Once low pressure is reached, reduce the heat to stabilise the pressure and cook for 5 minutes, or until the vegetables are tender.

4 Remove the cooker from the heat and release the pressure using the natural release method. Remove the lid carefully.

5 Stir in the remaining coconut milk and season to taste with salt and freshly ground black pepper.

6 Serve the curry garnished with coriander, accompanied by rice.

NOTE: Tamarind purée is available from the Asian section of larger supermarkets and Asian grocery stores. Don't confuse it with tamarind pulp, which needs to be softened in water before using.

Mushroom risotto

Preparation time 10 minutes • **Cooking time** 22 minutes • **Serves** 4

2 tablespoons olive oil
40 g (1½ oz) butter
200 g (7 oz) button mushrooms, sliced
3 garlic cloves, crushed
1 brown onion, diced
150 g (5½ oz) mushroom flats, trimmed and
  cut into large chunks

330 g (11½ oz/1½ cups) arborio rice
125 ml (4 fl oz/½ cup) dry white wine
875 ml (30 fl oz/3½ cups) good-quality purchased
  or homemade vegetable stock (see page 18)
135 g (4¾ oz/1 cup) finely grated parmesan
  cheese
chopped flat-leaf (Italian) parsley leaves, to garnish

1 Heat half the oil and half the butter in a 6 litre (210 fl oz) pressure cooker over medium–high heat and cook the button mushrooms for 5 minutes, or until browned and tender. Stir in the garlic and cook for 1 minute, or until aromatic. Remove the mushrooms from the cooker, cover loosely with foil to keep warm and set aside.

2 Heat the remaining oil in the cooker over medium–high heat and cook the onion and other mushrooms for 5–8 minutes, stirring occasionally, until softened. Stir in the rice and cook for 1 minute. Pour in the wine and keep stirring until the wine is nearly absorbed. Pour in the stock and stir well.

3 Lock the lid in place and bring the cooker to high pressure over high heat. Once high pressure is reached, reduce the heat to stabilise the pressure and cook for 6 minutes, or until the rice is tender.

4 Remove the cooker from the heat and release the pressure using the quick release method. Remove the lid carefully.

5 Season the risotto to taste with freshly ground black pepper, then stir in the parmesan and the remaining butter. Cover and stand for 1 minute, or until the butter has melted.

6 Serve topped with the button mushrooms and garnished with parsley.

NOTE: You can use any mushrooms in this dish — try shiitake mushrooms in place of the button mushrooms, and portobello mushrooms instead of the mushroom flats.

SEAFOOD

Portuguese seafood stew

Preparation time 20 minutes (+ 10 minutes infusing) • **Cooking time** 7 minutes • **Serves** 4

¼ teaspoon saffron threads (see Note)
1 leek, pale section only, rinsed well and
  chopped into 1 cm (½ inch) pieces
1 chorizo sausage, halved and cut into 1 cm
  (½ inch) slices
½ teaspoon smoked or mild paprika
1 red capsicum (pepper), cut into 1.5 cm
  (⅝ inch) chunks
400 g (14 oz) tin chopped tomatoes

60 ml (2 fl oz/¼ cup) white wine
600 g (1 lb 5 oz) large raw king prawns (shrimp),
  peeled and deveined, leaving the tails intact
500 g (1 lb 2 oz) thick firm white fish fillets,
  cut into 3 cm (1¼ inch) chunks
2 tablespoons finely snipped chives
crusty bread, to serve
green salad, to serve

1 Combine the saffron and 1 tablespoon of very hot water in a small bowl. Set aside for 10 minutes to infuse.

2 Place the leek, chorizo, paprika, capsicum, tomatoes and wine in a 6 litre (210 fl oz) pressure cooker. Add the saffron water and mix well. Season with salt and freshly ground black pepper.

3 Lock the lid in place and bring the cooker to high pressure over high heat. Once high pressure is reached, reduce the heat to stabilise the pressure and cook for 5 minutes. Remove the cooker from the heat and release the pressure using the quick release method. Remove the lid carefully.

4 Add the prawns and fish to the cooker and briefly stir to combine, then replace the lid immediately and lock in place. Bring the cooker to low pressure

over high heat. Once low pressure is reached, reduce the heat to stabilise the pressure and cook for 2 minutes, or until the seafood is just cooked.

5 Remove the cooker from the heat and release the pressure using the quick release method. Remove the lid carefully.

6 Ladle the stew into wide shallow serving bowls and sprinkle with the chives. Serve with crusty bread and a green salad.

NOTE: Saffron imparts a lovely yellowish-orange hue to dishes. It is best to soak it in a little liquid before using it in a recipe. The saffron will dissolve, allowing its colour to blend evenly through the finished dish.

Madras fish and potato curry

Preparation time 10 minutes • **Cooking time** 22 minutes • **Serves** 4

1 tablespoon vegetable oil
2 brown onions, thinly sliced
2 large ripe tomatoes, diced
¼ cup fresh curry leaves (optional)
270 ml (9½ fl oz) tin coconut milk
125 ml (4 fl oz/½ cup) good-quality purchased
   or homemade fish stock (see page 21)
2 tablespoons madras curry paste
1 tablespoon finely grated fresh ginger

1 kg (2 lb 4 oz) all-purpose potatoes, peeled
   and cut into 4 cm (1½ inch) chunks
700 g (1 lb 9 oz) firm white fish fillets, cut into
   4 cm (1½ inch) chunks
1 long red chilli, finely chopped
chopped coriander (cilantro) leaves, to garnish
cooked basmati rice (see page 12), to serve

1 Heat the oil in a 6 litre (210 fl oz) pressure cooker over medium–high heat and cook the onion, stirring occasionally, for 7 minutes, or until well browned.

2 Reduce the heat to medium. Add the tomato and curry leaves and simmer for 2 minutes, or until the tomato breaks down, scraping the base of the pot well to scrape off any cooked-on bits. Stir in the coconut milk, stock, curry paste and ginger. Add the potato and stir well.

3 Lock the lid in place and bring the cooker to high pressure over medium heat. Once high pressure is reached, reduce the heat to stabilise the pressure and cook for 10 minutes, or until the potato is almost tender.

4 Remove the cooker from the heat and release the pressure using the quick release method. Remove the lid carefully.

5 Add the fish, replace the lid immediately and lock in place. Bring the cooker to low pressure over high heat. Once low pressure is reached, reduce the heat to stabilise the pressure and cook for 3 minutes, or until the fish is just cooked.

6 Remove the cooker from the heat and release the pressure using the quick release method. Remove the lid carefully.

7 Season the curry with salt and freshly ground black pepper if required. Serve garnished with the chilli and coriander, with rice on the side.

Salmon with shallot butter sauce

Preparation time 10 minutes • **Cooking time** 6 minutes • **Serves** 4

125 ml (4 fl oz/½ cup) white wine
2 tablespoons lemon juice
2 shallots, finely chopped
4 (about 600 g/1 lb 5 oz) skinless salmon fillets

125 g (4½ oz) cold butter, diced
2 tablespoons finely snipped chives
steamed potatoes, to serve
steamed spinach, to serve

1 Put the wine, lemon juice and shallot in a 6 litre (210 fl oz) pressure cooker and place a trivet on the base. Place the salmon in a single layer in an oiled steamer basket (see Notes) and lower it into the cooker on top of the trivet.

2 Lock the lid in place and bring the cooker to low pressure over high heat. Once low pressure is reached, reduce the heat to stabilise the pressure and cook for 5 minutes, or until the salmon is just cooked through.

3 Remove the cooker from the heat and release the pressure using the quick release method. Remove the lid carefully.

4 Remove the steamer basket from the cooker, then transfer the salmon to a plate and cover loosely with foil to keep warm. Remove the trivet from the cooker.

5 Place the cooker over high heat and boil the wine mixture, uncovered, for 1 minute, or until reduced to about 80 ml (2½ fl oz/⅓ cup). Reduce the heat and gradually whisk in the butter, a piece at a time, until the sauce is smooth and slightly thickened. Season with salt and freshly ground black pepper.

6 Arrange the salmon on serving plates. Spoon the sauce over and sprinkle with the chives. Serve with steamed potatoes and spinach.

NOTES: Try not to overcrowd the steamer basket, so that there's a bit of space between each salmon fillet. The wider your pressure cooker, the easier this will be.

We used a portion of salmon from the centre of the fillet, which was about 4 cm (1½ inches) thick. If using slightly thinner or thicker portions, adjust the cooking time accordingly.

Saffron risotto with prawns

Preparation time 15 minutes • **Cooking time** 12 minutes • **Serves** 4

2 tablespoons olive oil
1 brown onion, diced
330 g (11½ oz/1½ cups) arborio rice
125 ml (4 fl oz/½ cup) white wine
750 ml (26 fl oz/3 cups) good-quality purchased
   or homemade fish stock (see page 21)

a pinch of saffron threads
40 g (1½ oz) butter
700 g (1 lb 9 oz) raw king prawns (shrimp),
   peeled and deveined, leaving the tails intact
3 garlic cloves, finely chopped
chopped flat-leaf (Italian) parsley leaves, to garnish

1 Heat half the oil in a 6 litre (210 fl oz) pressure cooker over medium–high heat and cook the onion with a pinch of salt for 3–4 minutes, or until softened. Stir in the rice and cook for 1 minute. Pour in the wine and keep stirring for 1 minute, or until the wine is nearly absorbed. Add the stock, saffron and 125 ml (4 fl oz/½ cup) water and stir well.

2 Lock the lid in place and bring the cooker to high pressure over high heat. Once high pressure is reached, reduce the heat to stabilise the pressure and cook for 6 minutes, or until the rice is tender.

3 Remove the cooker from the heat and release the pressure using the quick release method. Remove the lid carefully. Stir in the butter, then cover and stand for 1 minute, or until the butter has melted.

4 Meanwhile, heat the remaining oil in a large frying pan over high heat. Cook the prawns for 2 minutes, or until pink and just cooked through. Season to taste with salt and freshly ground black pepper, then stir in the garlic and cook until aromatic.

5 Divide the risotto among wide shallow serving bowls. Top with the prawns, sprinkle with black pepper, garnish with parsley and serve.

NOTE: You could also stir 100 g (3½ oz) baby spinach leaves into the rice when adding the butter.

Sides

Braised potatoes with white wine, onion and sage

Preparation time 10 minutes • **Cooking time** 8 minutes • **Serves** 4–6

750 g (1 lb 10 oz) potatoes, peeled and cut
    into 2 cm (¾ inch) thick slices
1 brown onion, halved and thinly sliced
2 tablespoons olive oil
2 tablespoons white wine

1 tablespoon coarsely shredded sage leaves
1 teaspoon salt
crisp sage leaves (see Notes), to serve (optional)
finely grated parmesan cheese, to serve

---

1 Place the potato, onion, oil, wine, sage and salt in a 6 litre (210 fl oz) pressure cooker. Pour in 80 ml (2½ fl oz/⅓ cup) water and stir well.

2 Lock the lid in place and bring the cooker to low pressure over medium heat. Once low pressure is reached, reduce the heat to stabilise the pressure and cook for 8 minutes, or until the potato is tender.

3 Remove the cooker from the heat and release the pressure using the natural release method. Remove the lid carefully.

4 Serve the potatoes immediately, drizzled with the sauce and sprinkled with crisp sage leaves, if desired, and some parmesan.

NOTES: To make crisp sage leaves, heat 40 g (1½ oz) butter in a frying pan over medium–high heat until foaming. Add the sage leaves and cook for 1 minute, or until crisp. Drain on paper towels.

    These potatoes are terrific with grilled (broiled) or steamed fish. You can try many combinations by changing the herbs or adding a chopped tomato.

Dhal

Preparation time 10 minutes • **Cooking time** 25 minutes • **Serves** 4

60 g (2¼ oz) ghee
2 brown onions, thinly sliced
3 garlic cloves, crushed
205 g (7¼ oz/1 cup) split red lentils, rinsed
and drained

1 long red chilli, seeded and finely chopped
1 teaspoon cumin seeds
½ teaspoon ground turmeric
1 tablespoon lemon juice
1 long green chilli, seeded and finely chopped

1 Melt the ghee in a 6 litre (210 fl oz) pressure cooker over medium–high heat and cook the onion, stirring occasionally, for 10 minutes, or until well browned. Remove half the onion and set aside.

2 Stir in the garlic and cook for 1 minute, or until aromatic. Add the lentils, red chilli, spices and 560 ml (19¼ fl oz/2¼ cups) water and stir well.

3 Lock the lid in place and bring the cooker to low pressure over high heat. Once low pressure is reached, reduce the heat to stabilise the pressure and cook for 14 minutes.

4 Remove the cooker from the heat and release the pressure using the natural release method. Remove the lid carefully.

5 Stir in the lemon juice and season to taste with salt and freshly ground black pepper. Serve topped with the reserved onion and sprinkled with the green chilli.

Stuffed eggplant

Preparation time 15 minutes (+ 5 minutes cooling) • **Cooking time** 15 minutes • **Serves** 4

2 small (about 350 g/12 oz each) eggplants
 (aubergines)
80 ml (2½ fl oz/⅓ cup) olive oil
1 large brown onion, finely chopped
3 garlic cloves, finely chopped
5 drained anchovy fillets, coarsely chopped
¼ cup parsley leaves, finely chopped

60 g (2¼ oz/1 cup, lightly packed) fresh
 breadcrumbs
35 g (1¼ oz/¼ cup) finely grated parmesan
 cheese
50 g (1¾ oz/⅓ cup) pine nuts, toasted
400 g (14 oz) tin chopped tomatoes
12 basil leaves, plus extra, to garnish

1 Cut the eggplants in half lengthways and scoop out the flesh, leaving a 1 cm (½ inch) border. Brush the eggplant halves inside and out with 1 tablespoon of the oil. Chop the flesh finely.

2 Heat another 1 tablespoon of the oil in a 6 litre (210 fl oz) pressure cooker over medium heat and cook the onion and garlic for 5 minutes, or until the onion has softened. Remove half the mixture and set aside.

3 Add the remaining oil, chopped eggplant, anchovy, parsley and breadcrumbs and cook, stirring, for 5 minutes, or until the eggplant is tender. Remove the mixture from the cooker and allow to cool for 5 minutes. Stir the parmesan and half the pine nuts through and season to taste with salt and freshly ground black pepper.

4 Spray a steamer basket with a little oil. Fill the eggplant halves with the breadcrumb mixture and arrange in the steamer basket, in two layers if necessary.

5 Return the reserved onion mixture to the pressure cooker, along with the tomatoes, basil and 80 ml (2½ fl oz/⅓ cup) water. Season to taste. Place a trivet inside the cooker and place the steamer basket on top.

6 Lock the lid in place and bring the cooker to low pressure over medium heat. Once low pressure is reached, reduce the heat to stabilise the pressure and cook for 5 minutes, or until the eggplant is tender. Release the pressure using the quick release method. Remove the lid carefully.

7 Carefully remove the eggplant halves from the steamer basket and arrange on a serving plate. Spoon the sauce over the top, sprinkle with the remaining pine nuts, garnish with extra basil and serve.

Mixed beans with tofu

Preparation time 10 minutes • **Cooking time** 2 minutes • **Serves** 4

150 g (5½ oz) firm tofu
1 tablespoon caster (superfine) sugar
1 tablespoon soy sauce
2 teaspoons mirin (see Note)

1 teaspoon sesame oil
400 g (14 oz) green beans, trimmed
2 teaspoons sesame seeds, toasted

1 Cut the tofu into 2 cm (¾ inch) cubes and place in a small heatproof bowl.

2 In a large bowl, combine the sugar, soy sauce, mirin and sesame oil. Stir until the sugar has dissolved, then pour over the tofu.

3 Pour 250 ml (9 fl oz/1 cup) water into a 6 litre (210 fl oz) pressure cooker and place a trivet over the base. Spread the beans in a steamer basket and place it on the trivet. Place the bowl of tofu on top of the beans.

4 Lock the lid in place and bring the cooker to low pressure over high heat. Once low pressure is reached, reduce the heat to stabilise the pressure and cook for 2 minutes, or until the beans are just tender.

5 Remove the cooker from the heat and release the pressure using the quick release method. Remove the lid carefully.

6 Using tongs, transfer the tofu and beans to a serving dish. Drizzle with the dressing, sprinkle with the sesame seeds and serve.

NOTE: Mirin is a sweet wine made from glutinous rice. It is golden in colour, has a low alcohol content and adds sweetness and flavour to dishes. You will find it in the Asian section of supermarkets and in Asian grocery stores.

Quick tomato passata

Preparation time 10 minutes • **Cooking time** 15 minutes • **Makes** 1.25 litres (44 fl oz/5 cups)

2 tablespoons extra virgin olive oil
½ brown onion, chopped
½ small carrot, chopped
1 celery stalk, chopped

3 garlic cloves, chopped
1 teaspoon dried oregano
1 teaspoon salt
3 x 400 g (14 oz) tins chopped tomatoes

1 Heat the oil in a 6 litre (210 fl oz) pressure cooker over medium heat. Add all the ingredients except the tomatoes and cook, stirring occasionally, for 5 minutes, or until the vegetables begin to soften. Add the tomatoes, stir well and season with freshly ground black pepper.

2 Lock the lid in place and bring the cooker to high pressure over medium heat. Once high pressure is reached, reduce the heat to stabilise the pressure and cook for 5 minutes. Remove the cooker from the heat and release the pressure using the quick release method. Remove the lid carefully.

3 Return the cooker to medium heat and simmer for 4–5 minutes, or until the sauce thickens slightly. Taste and season if necessary.

4 If desired, purée the passata using a stick blender to the desired consistency.

NOTES: This sauce is delicious served with grilled (broiled) or barbecued chicken or fish. It can also be used as a base for pasta sauces, braises and casseroles, or as a pizza sauce.

This passata will keep in an airtight container in the refrigerator for up to 4 days, or in the freezer for up to 3 months.

Cheesy cauliflower and potato mash with crisp bacon

Preparation time 15 minutes • **Cooking time** 8 minutes • **Serves** 6

1 tablespoon olive oil
2 bacon slices, trimmed and finely chopped
400 g (14 oz) desiree potatoes, peeled and cut
    into 2 cm (³/₄ inch) chunks
1 small (about 800 g/1 lb 12 oz) cauliflower,
    core removed, cut into large florets

60 ml (2 fl oz/¼ cup) pouring (whipping) cream
40 g (1½ oz) butter
75 g (2½ oz/¾ cup) finely grated cheddar cheese
5–6 drops Tabasco sauce, or to taste (optional)

1 Heat the oil in a 6 litre (210 fl oz) pressure cooker over medium–high heat and cook the bacon, stirring often, for 3 minutes, or until crisp. Remove from the cooker using a slotted spoon, drain on paper towels and set aside.

2 Lightly oil a pressure cooker steamer basket. Place the potato in the basket, then arrange the cauliflower florets over the top. Sprinkle with a pinch of salt.

3 Pour 250 ml (9 fl oz/1 cup) water into the pressure cooker and place a trivet over the base. Place the steamer basket on the trivet.

4 Lock the lid in place and bring the cooker to high pressure over high heat. Once high pressure is reached, reduce the heat to stabilise the pressure and cook for 5 minutes, or until the potato and cauliflower are tender.

5 Remove the cooker from the heat and release the pressure using the quick release method. Remove the lid carefully. Remove the steamer basket from the cooker and allow to drain for 1 minute.

6 Transfer the potato and cauliflower to a large bowl and coarsely mash. Add the cream and butter and mash until smooth. Stir in the cheese and Tabasco, if desired, then season to taste with salt and freshly ground black pepper.

7 Serve the mash topped with the crisp bacon.

Zucchini with mint and feta

Preparation time 10 minutes • **Cooking time** 2 minutes • **Serves** 4

**3 (about 450 g/1 lb) zucchini (courgettes),
   thickly sliced on the diagonal**
1 tablespoon extra virgin olive oil

2 teaspoons white balsamic vinegar (see Notes)
¼ cup torn mint leaves
30 g (1 oz) Greek feta cheese, crumbled

1 Pour 250 ml (9 fl oz/1 cup) water into a 6 litre (210 fl oz) pressure cooker and place a trivet over the base. Place the zucchini in a steamer basket and place it on the trivet.

2 Lock the lid in place and bring the cooker to low pressure over high heat. Once low pressure is reached, reduce the heat to stabilise the pressure and cook for 1½ minutes, or until the zucchini is just tender.

3 Remove the cooker from the heat and release the pressure using the quick release method. Remove the lid carefully.

4 Transfer the zucchini to a bowl. Add the oil, vinegar and half the mint. Season to taste with salt and freshly ground black pepper and gently toss to coat.

5 Top with the feta and remaining mint and serve.

NOTES: White balsamic vinegar is also sometimes called white balsamic condiment and can be found in the vinegar section of larger supermarkets, as well as delicatessens and gourmet food stores.

You can serve this dish warm or at room temperature. If left to stand too long, however, the mint in the dressing tends to go brown.

Lemon and rocket risotto

Preparation time 10 minutes • **Cooking time** 12 minutes • **Serves** 6

1 tablespoon olive oil
1 brown onion, diced
330 g (11½ oz/1½ cups) arborio rice
125 ml (4 fl oz/½ cup) white wine
875 ml (30 fl oz/3½ cups) good-quality purchased or homemade vegetable stock (see page 18)
1 bunch (about 100 g/3½ oz) rocket (arugula), trimmed and coarsely chopped

70 g (2½ oz/½ cup) finely grated parmesan cheese
1 tablespoon finely grated lemon zest
1 tablespoon lemon juice
25 g (1 oz) butter, chopped

1 Heat the oil in a 6 litre (210 fl oz) pressure cooker over medium heat and cook the onion with a pinch of salt for 3–4 minutes, or until softened. Stir in the rice and cook for 1 minute. Pour in the wine and keep stirring for 1 minute, or until the wine is nearly absorbed. Pour in the stock and stir well.

2 Lock the lid in place and bring the cooker to high pressure over high heat. Once high pressure is reached, reduce the heat to stabilise the pressure and cook for 6 minutes, or until the rice is tender.

3 Remove the cooker from the heat and release the pressure using the quick release method. Remove the lid carefully.

4 Stir in the remaining ingredients, reserving some of the rocket for garnishing. Cover and stand for 1 minute, or until the butter has melted and the rocket has wilted.

5 Season to taste with salt and freshly ground black pepper and serve immediately, garnished with the remaining rocket.

NOTE: This risotto is delicious as a starter, or served alongside grilled (broiled) fish, lamb chops or roasted chicken.

Potato gratin with chives and paprika

Preparation time 15 minutes • **Cooking time** 15 minutes • **Serves** 4

butter, for greasing
80 ml (2½ fl oz/⅓ cup) pouring (whipping) cream
1 teaspoon dijon mustard
500 g (1 lb 2 oz) desiree potatoes, peeled and
    sliced into 3 mm (⅛ inch) thick rounds

2 tablespoons finely snipped chives
50 g (1¾ oz/⅓ cup) finely grated
    parmesan cheese
½ teaspoon sweet or mild paprika

1 Lightly grease a shallow 16 cm (6¼ inch) square ovenproof ceramic dish. Combine the cream and mustard in a jug and set aside. Arrange half the potato slices in the dish, slightly overlapping, to cover the base. Season with salt and freshly ground black pepper, pour half the cream mixture over, then scatter with half of the chives. Arrange the remaining potato slices on top, season again and pour the remaining cream mixture over. Cover tightly with foil.

2 Pour 375 ml (13 fl oz/1½ cups) water into an 8 litre (280 fl oz) pressure cooker and place a trivet over the base. Fold a tea towel (dish towel) lengthways into thirds, set it on a flat surface and place the dish with the potatoes in the centre. Lift up the ends of the tea towel to form a sling, then lower the dish onto the trivet. Fold the tea towel edges over the top of the foil.

3 Lock the lid in place and bring the cooker to high pressure over high heat. Once high pressure is reached, reduce the heat to stabilise the pressure and cook for 12 minutes, or until the potato is tender.

4 Meanwhile, preheat the grill (broiler) to high.

5 Remove the cooker from the heat and release the pressure using the quick release method. Remove the lid carefully. Lift the edges of the tea towel and rest them on the edge of the cooker to cool slightly. Remove the dish from the cooker and and remove the foil.

6 Sprinkle the gratin with the parmesan and the paprika. Grill (broil) for 2–3 minutes, or until the cheese is golden brown. Sprinkle with the remaining chives and serve.

Warm beetroot and carrot salad

Preparation time 10 minutes • **Cooking time** 12 minutes • **Serves** 4

3–4 small beetroot (beets)
500 ml (17 fl oz/2 cups) good-quality purchased
    or homemade chicken stock (see page 14),
    or water
60 g (2¼ oz) butter
2 tablespoons chopped flat-leaf (Italian)
    parsley leaves

2 teaspoons red wine vinegar
400 g (14 oz) small carrots, cut into 10 cm (4 inch)
    lengths, then quartered lengthways
1 tablespoon honey

1 Trim and peel the beetroot, then cut into 1 cm (½ inch) thick wedges. Place in an 8 litre (280 fl oz) pressure cooker with 435 ml (15¼ fl oz/1¾ cups) of the stock or water, 20 g (¾ oz) of the butter, half the parsley and ½ teaspoon of the vinegar. Season well with salt and freshly ground black pepper.

2 Lock the lid in place and bring the cooker to high pressure over high heat. Once high pressure is reached, reduce the heat to stabilise the pressure and cook for 4 minutes.

3 Meanwhile, arrange the carrot in an 18 cm (7 inch) heatproof dish. Add the remaining butter, remaining stock or water and drizzle with the honey. Season well.

4 Remove the cooker from the heat and release the pressure using the quick release method. Remove the lid carefully. Place a trivet inside the cooker, over the beetroot. Place the heatproof dish on the trivet. Replace the lid immediately and lock in place.

5 Bring the cooker back to high pressure over high heat. Once high pressure is reached, reduce the heat to stabilise the pressure and cook for 8 minutes, or until the vegetables are tender. Remove the cooker from the heat and release the pressure using the quick release method. Remove the lid carefully.

6 Remove the carrot and beetroot separately, draining and reserving any juices. Place the beetroot, carrot and remaining parsely in a bowl. Mix 60 ml (2 fl oz/¼ cup) of the reserved carrot liquid with the remaining vinegar. Drizzle the dressing over the vegetables, toss to coat in the dressing and serve warm.

NOTE: This salad is delicious with roasted or barbecued lamb, beef, pork, chicken or duck.

Corn on the cob with garlic and parsley butter

Preparation time 10 minutes • **Cooking time** 3 minutes • **Serves** 6

6 corn cobs, husks and silks removed

GARLIC AND PARSLEY BUTTER
80 g (2¾ oz) butter, softened
2 garlic cloves, crushed
2 tablespoons finely chopped flat-leaf (Italian)
  parsley leaves

1 Pour 250 ml (9 fl oz/1 cup) water into a 6 litre (210 fl oz) pressure cooker and place a trivet over the base. Place the corn in a steamer basket and place it on the trivet.

2 Lock the lid in place and bring the cooker to low pressure over high heat. Once low pressure is reached, reduce the heat to stabilise the pressure and cook for 3 minutes, or until the corn is tender.

3 Meanwhile, combine the butter, garlic and parsley in a small bowl.

4 Remove the cooker from the heat and release the pressure using the quick release method. Remove the lid carefully.

5 Serve the corn hot, topped with the garlic and parsley butter.

NOTE: If you have the time and prefer to make a log with the butter, place the flavoured butter on a piece of plastic wrap, shape it into a 6 cm (2½ inch) log and wrap tightly. Freeze for 30 minutes, or until firm.

Butter variations

Tarragon and mustard butter: Combine 80 g (2¾ oz) softened salted butter with 2 teaspoons wholegrain mustard and 2 teaspoons finely chopped tarragon.

Chilli and anchovy butter: Combine 80 g (2¾ oz) softened salted butter with 4 drained and finely chopped anchovy fillets, 1 teaspoon chilli flakes and 1 teaspoon finely grated lemon zest.

Warm pearl barley and herb salad

Preparation time 10 minutes • **Cooking time** 20 minutes • **Serves** 6

300 g (10½ oz/1½ cups) pearl barley
500 ml (17 fl oz/2 cups) good-quality purchased
  or homemade chicken stock (see page 14)
1 Lebanese (short) cucumber, diced
¼ red onion, finely chopped
1 cup finely chopped flat-leaf (Italian) parsley
  leaves

½ cup finely chopped mint leaves, plus
  extra leaves, to garnish
60 ml (2 fl oz/¼ cup) extra virgin olive oil
1½ tablespoons lemon juice

1 Combine the barley, stock and 250 ml (9 fl oz/ 1 cup) water in a 6 litre (210 fl oz) pressure cooker and stir well.

2 Lock the lid in place and bring the cooker to high pressure over high heat. Once high pressure is reached, reduce the heat to stabilise the pressure and cook for 20 minutes, or until the barley is tender.

3 Remove the cooker from the heat and release the pressure using the quick release method. Remove the lid carefully.

4 Drain the barley and place in a large bowl with the remaining ingredients. Season to taste with salt and freshly ground black pepper. Toss to combine and serve garnished with extra mint.

Lebanese pilaff

Preparation time 10 minutes (+ 5 minutes standing) • **Cooking time** 12 minutes • **Serves** 4–6

2 tablespoons olive oil
1 brown onion, diced
300 g (10½ oz/1½ cups) basmati rice
1 teaspoon ground cinnamon
1 teaspoon ground allspice
560 ml (19¼ fl oz/2¼ cups) good-quality
   purchased or homemade chicken stock
   (see page 14)

400 g (14 oz) tin chickpeas, rinsed and drained
2 tablespoons pine nuts, toasted
2 tablespoons slivered or flaked almonds, toasted
2 tablespoons finely chopped mint leaves

1 Heat the oil in a 6 litre (210 fl oz) pressure cooker over medium heat and cook the onion, stirring, for 3–4 minutes, or until softened. Stir in the rice and cook for 1 minute. Stir in the spices and cook for 1 minute, or until aromatic. Add the stock and chickpeas and stir well.

2 Lock the lid in place and bring the cooker to low pressure over high heat. Once low pressure is reached, reduce the heat to stabilise the pressure and cook for 6 minutes, or until the rice is tender.

3 Remove the cooker from the heat and release the pressure using the natural release method. Remove the lid carefully. Stir the rice with a fork to separate the grains, replace the lid immediately and lock in place. Stand for 5 minutes.

4 Remove the lid carefully and fluff up the grains with a fork. Transfer to a large serving bowl and serve sprinkled with the pine nuts, almonds and mint.

NOTE: This pilaff is great served with chicken or lamb kebabs and a dollop of yoghurt.

Braised borlotti beans with tomato and rosemary

Preparation time 5 minutes • **Cooking time** 37 minutes • **Serves** 6

300 g (10½ oz/1½ cups) dried borlotti
  (cranberry) beans, rinsed and drained
1 teaspoon salt
2 tablespoons olive oil
1 brown onion, chopped

3 garlic cloves, thinly sliced
400 g (14 oz) tin chopped tomatoes
80 ml (2½ fl oz/⅓ cup) red wine
1 tablespoon rosemary leaves, plus extra sprigs,
  to garnish

---

1 Combine the beans, salt and 1 litre (35 fl oz/ 4 cups) water in a 6 litre (210 fl oz) pressure cooker.

2 Lock the lid in place and bring the cooker to high pressure over high heat. Once high pressure is reached, reduce the heat to stabilise the pressure and cook for 2 minutes.

3 Remove the cooker from the heat and release the pressure using the quick release method. Remove the lid carefully. Drain and rinse the beans.

4 Wipe out the cooker and place over medium heat. Heat the oil in the cooker and cook the onion, stirring occasionally, for 3–4 minutes, or until softened. Stir in the garlic and cook for 1 minute, or until aromatic. Return the beans to the cooker with the tomatoes, wine, rosemary and 375 ml (13 fl oz/1½ cups) water and stir well.

5 Lock the lid in place and bring the cooker to high pressure over high heat. Once high pressure is reached, reduce the heat to stabilise the pressure and cook for 30 minutes, or until the beans are tender.

6 Remove the cooker from the heat and release the pressure using the natural release method. Remove the lid carefully.

7 Season the beans well with salt and freshly ground black pepper. Serve warm, garnished with extra rosemary sprigs.

NOTE: These beans are delicious served with roast lamb or chargrilled lamb chops.

Desserts

Upside-down blackberry puddings

Preparation time 10 minutes • **Cooking time** 18 minutes • **Makes** 4

50 g (1¾ oz) unsalted butter, at room
  temperature, plus extra, for greasing
150 g (5½ oz) frozen blackberries
110 g (3¾ oz/½ cup) caster (superfine) sugar
60 ml (2 fl oz/¼ cup) milk
finely grated zest of 1 lime

2 eggs
¼ teaspoon baking powder
100 g (3½ oz/⅔ cup) self-raising flour
icing (confectioners') sugar, for dusting
cream, to serve

1 Lightly grease four 250 ml (9 fl oz/1 cup) ramekins or dariole moulds with butter. Divide the blackberries among them.

2 Place the remaining ingredients, except the icing sugar and cream, in a food processor and process for 3 seconds. Scrape down the side and process until the mixture is just combined. Divide the mixture evenly among the ramekins and smooth the tops. Cover each ramekin tightly with foil and place in a steamer basket, stacking them in two layers if necessary.

3 Pour 500 ml (17 fl oz/2 cups) water into an 8 litre (280 fl oz) pressure cooker and place a trivet over the base. Place the steamer basket on the trivet.

4 Lock the lid in place and bring the cooker to high pressure over high heat. Once high pressure is reached, reduce the heat to stabilise the pressure and cook for 18 minutes, or until the puddings are just cooked through.

5 Remove the cooker from the heat and release the pressure using the natural release method. Remove the lid carefully.

6 Remove the steamer basket from the cooker and remove the foil from the ramekins. Invert each pudding onto a plate. Dust with icing sugar and serve warm, drizzled with cream.

Poached pears in sweet sherry

Preparation time 15 minutes • **Cooking time** 20 minutes • **Serves** 6

100 g (3½ oz/½ cup, lightly packed) brown sugar
375 ml (13 fl oz/1½ cups) sweet sherry
6 small (about 150 g/5½ oz each) firm ripe pears
2 lime peel strips, each about 2 cm (¾ inch)
   wide, white pith removed
1 tablespoon lime juice

½ teaspoon natural almond extract
2 cinnamon sticks
6 whole cloves
a pinch of freshly grated nutmeg
vanilla ice cream, to serve

1 Combine the sugar, sherry and 125 ml (4 fl oz/½ cup) water in a 6 litre (210 fl oz) pressure cooker. Place over medium heat and stir until the sugar has dissolved. Remove from the heat.

2 Peel the pears and halve them lengthways, leaving the stems attached. Use a teaspoon, melon baller or small sharp knife to remove the core from each half, placing the pear halves in the sherry syrup as you go so they don't discolour.

3 Add the remaining ingredients (except the ice cream) to the pressure cooker and stir gently to combine. Lock the lid in place and bring the cooker to low pressure over high heat. Once low pressure is reached, reduce the heat to stabilise the pressure and cook for 8 minutes, or until the pears are just tender.

4 Remove the cooker from the heat and release the pressure using the natural release method. Remove the lid carefully. Using a slotted spoon, remove the pears from the syrup and set aside.

5 Place the cooker over medium–high heat and gently boil the syrup, uncovered, for 12 minutes, or until reduced to about 185 ml (6 fl oz/¾ cup).

6 Serve the pears drizzled with the syrup, and accompanied by ice cream.

Rice pudding with mixed berries

Preparation time 5 minutes • **Cooking time** 12 minutes • **Serves** 6

500 ml (17 fl oz/2 cups) milk
220 g (7¾ oz/1 cup) medium-grain white rice
75 g (2½ oz/⅓ cup) caster (superfine) sugar

½ vanilla bean, split lengthways,
  seeds scraped
500 g (1 lb 2 oz) mixed fresh berries (see Note)

1 Combine the milk, rice, sugar and vanilla bean and seeds in a 6 litre (210 fl oz) pressure cooker. Pour in 435 ml (15¼ fl oz/1¾ cups) water and stir well.

2 Lock the lid in place and bring the cooker to high pressure over high heat. Once high pressure is reached, reduce the heat to stabilise the pressure and cook for 12 minutes, or until the rice is just tender.

3 Remove the cooker from the heat and release the pressure using the natural release method. Remove the lid carefully.

4 Serve the puddings warm, topped with the berries.

NOTE: We used a mixture of strawberries, raspberries and blueberries, but you could also serve this creamy rice with wedges of stone fruit or poached pears. You can also spoon the rice into ramekins, refrigerate until chilled, and serve sprinkled with ground cinnamon.

Nectarines with vanilla syrup

Preparation time 10 minutes (+ cooling time) • **Cooking time** 7 minutes • **Serves** 8

250 ml (9 fl oz/1 cup) white wine
110 g (3¾ oz/½ cup) caster (superfine) sugar
½ vanilla bean, split lengthways, seeds scraped
8 (about 150 g/5½ oz each) firm, ripe nectarines
  (see Note)

thick (double/heavy) cream or Greek-style
  yoghurt, to serve

1 Combine the wine, sugar and vanilla bean and seeds in an 8 litre (280 fl oz) pressure cooker. Pour in 250 ml (9 fl oz/1 cup) water and stir over medium heat until the sugar has dissolved. Add the whole nectarines and turn to coat them in the syrup. Make sure the fruit isn't touching the side of the cooker.

2 Lock the lid in place and bring the cooker to high pressure over high heat. Once high pressure is reached, reduce the heat to stabilise the pressure and cook for 3 minutes, or until the nectarines are just tender.

3 Remove the cooker from the heat and release the pressure using the natural release method. Remove the lid carefully.

4 Using a slotted spoon, immediately transfer the nectarines to a dish and set aside to cool. Once cooled, peel away and discard the skins.

5 Meanwhile, place the cooker over medium heat and gently boil the syrup, uncovered, for 3–4 minutes, or until it has reduced by one-third and is syrupy. Transfer the syrup to a heatproof jug and refrigerate until cooled.

6 Pour the syrup over the fruit. Serve with cream or yoghurt.

NOTE: You can use firm ripe peaches instead of the nectarines if desired.

Individual baked custards

Preparation time 10 minutes (+ 10 minutes cooling) • **Cooking time** 7 minutes • **Serves** 4

250 ml (9 fl oz/1 cup) thickened (whipping) cream
250 ml (9 fl oz/1 cup) milk
2 large eggs, lightly beaten
1 teaspoon natural vanilla extract

55 g (2 oz/¼ cup) caster (superfine) sugar
60 ml (2 fl oz/¼ cup) maple syrup
1 teaspoon finely grated orange zest
¼ teaspoon freshly grated nutmeg

1 Combine all the ingredients except the nutmeg in a large bowl and whisk lightly until just combined. Transfer the mixture to a jug, then divide evenly among four 250 ml (9 fl oz/1 cup) ramekins or dariole moulds. Cover each ramekin tightly with foil.

2 Pour 250 ml (9 fl oz/1 cup) water into an 8 litre (280 fl oz) pressure cooker and place a trivet over the base. Arrange the ramekins in a steamer basket, stacking them two layers high, if necessary. Set the steamer basket on the trivet.

3 Lock the lid in place and bring the cooker to high pressure over high heat. Once high pressure is reached, reduce the heat to stabilise the pressure and cook for 7 minutes, or until the custards are set but still very wobbly.

4 Remove the cooker from the heat and release the pressure using the natural release method. Remove the lid carefully. Remove the ramekins from the cooker and set aside for 5–10 minutes to cool slightly.

5 Serve the custards warm or at room temperature, sprinkled with the nutmeg.

NOTE: For firmer custards, refrigerate them for 3–4 hours before serving.

Chocolate and banana bread and butter pudding

Preparation time 10 minutes (+ 15 minutes soaking) • **Cooking time** 18 minutes • **Serves** 6

30 g (1 oz) softened butter, plus extra,
   for greasing
5 thick slices (about 260 g/9¼ oz) stale
   country-style white bread (see Note), crusts
   removed
1 firm ripe banana, cut into 1 cm (½ inch) rounds
60 g (2¼ oz) dark chocolate, half chopped, the
   remainder coarsely grated

3 eggs, at room temperature
60 g (2¼ oz/⅓ cup, lightly packed)
   brown sugar
1 teaspoon natural vanilla extract
330 ml (11¼ fl oz/1⅓ cups) milk
½ teaspoon ground cinnamon
whipped cream or ice cream, to serve

1 Lightly grease an 18 cm (7 inch) round cake tin with butter and set aside.

2 Spread the bread on both sides with the butter and cut into 3 cm (1¼ inch) cubes. Arrange half the bread in the cake tin and scatter with the banana slices. Sprinkle with the chopped chocolate, then cover with the remaining bread cubes.

3 Whisk the eggs with the sugar and vanilla until just combined. Heat the milk in a small saucepan until just simmering, then gradually whisk it into the egg mixture. Strain the mixture through a sieve, over the bread. Gently press down on the bread to ensure the top cubes are moistened. Set aside to soak for 15 minutes, or until the bread has absorbed most of the milk. Sprinkle the pudding with the cinnamon, then cover tightly with foil.

4 Pour 500 ml (17 fl oz/2 cups) water into an 8 litre (280 fl oz) pressure cooker and place a trivet over the base. Fold a tea towel (dish towel) lengthways into thirds and place the cake tin in the centre. Lift up the ends to form a sling, then lower the tin onto the trivet. Fold the tea towel ends over the top of the tin.

5 Lock the lid in place and bring the cooker to high pressure over high heat. Once high pressure is reached, reduce the heat to stabilise the pressure and cook for 18 minutes, or until the pudding is just set.

6 Remove the cooker from the heat and release the pressure using the natural release method. Remove the lid carefully. Lift the ends of the tea towel and drape them over the side of the cooker for a little while to cool slightly.

7 Remove the pudding from the cooker and remove the foil. Serve the pudding warm with a dollop of whipped cream or ice cream, and sprinkled with the grated chocolate.

NOTE: The bread needs to be very stale and dry for a successful pudding — make sure it is at least 4 days old. If you can find it, sourdough bread is an excellent choice.

Self-saucing chocolate and cherry pudding

Preparation time 15 minutes • **Cooking time** 25 minutes • **Serves** 4

30 g (1 oz) softened unsalted butter,
  plus extra, for greasing
425 g (15 oz) tin cherries in syrup, drained
  and halved, syrup reserved
50 g (1¾ oz/⅓ cup) self-raising flour
30 g (1 oz/¼ cup) unsweetened cocoa powder

¼ teaspoon baking powder
250 ml (9 fl oz/1 cup) milk
110 g (3¾ oz/½ cup) caster (superfine)
  sugar
2 eggs, at room temperature, separated
vanilla ice cream, to serve

1 Lightly grease a deep, 18 cm (7 inch) round cake tin with butter. Arrange the cherries in an even layer over the base of the tin. Sift the flour, cocoa powder and baking powder into a large bowl. Combine the milk and 60 ml (2 fl oz/¼ cup) of the reserved cherry syrup.

2 Beat the butter and sugar using electric beaters until light and fluffy. Beat in the egg yolks, one at a time, beating well after each addition. Use a balloon whisk to gently whisk in the dry ingredients, alternating with the milk mixture, until combined.

3 In a separate bowl, whisk the egg whites using an electric mixer with a whisk attachment until stiff peaks form. Gently fold the egg whites into the pudding mixture until just combined. Pour the mixture into the cake tin, smooth the surface and cover tightly with foil.

4 Pour 500 ml (17 fl oz/2 cups) water into an 8 litre (280 fl oz) pressure cooker and place a trivet over the base. Fold a tea towel (dish towel) lengthways into thirds and place the cake tin in the centre. Lift up the ends to form a sling, then lower the tin onto the trivet. Fold the tea towel ends over the top of the tin.

5 Lock the lid in place and bring the cooker to high pressure over high heat. Once high pressure is reached, reduce the heat to stabilise the pressure and cook for 25 minutes.

6 Remove the cooker from the heat and release the pressure using the natural release method. Remove the lid carefully. Lift the ends of the tea towel and drape them over the side of the cooker for a little while to cool slightly.

7 Remove the pudding from the cooker and remove the foil. The pudding should be slightly wobbly in the centre. Immediately scoop the pudding and sauce into serving bowls and serve with ice cream.

Raspberry swirl cheesecake

Preparation time 33 minutes (+ cooling + 4 hours chilling)
- **Cooking time** 35 minutes • **Serves** 10

250 g (9 oz) shredded wheat biscuits (cookies)
100 g (3½ oz) butter, melted
150 g (5½ oz) frozen raspberries
150 g (5½ oz/⅔ cup) caster (superfine) sugar

750 g (1 lb 10 oz/3¼ cups) cream cheese,
  softened
2 eggs
2 tablespoons lemon juice

---

1 Using a food processor, process the biscuits into fine crumbs. Combine the crumbs and melted butter. Press the crumb mixture into a 22 cm (8½ inch) spring-form cake tin, covering the base and 4 cm (1½ inches) up the side. Refrigerate the biscuit base while preparing the filling.

2 Place the raspberries in a small saucepan with 2 tablespoons of the sugar. Cook over medium heat for 5 minutes, breaking up the raspberries with a wooden spoon, until the sugar has dissolved and the raspberries are soft. Simmer for a futher 8 minutes, or until thickened. Pass the raspberry mixture through a sieve and discard the seeds. Refrigerate until cool.

3 Using electric beaters, beat the cream cheese and remaining sugar until smooth. Beat in the eggs, one at a time, then stir in the lemon juice. Spoon the cream cheese mixture into the prepared crust.

4 Drop tablespoons of the cooled raspberry mixture over the filling and swirl lightly with a small metal spatula or teaspoon. Wrap the whole cake tin tightly in foil, sealing well so any steam can't get in, but ensuring the foil doesn't touch the filling.

5 Pour 250 ml (9 fl oz/1 cup) water into a 6 litre (210 fl oz) pressure cooker (see Notes). Lower a trivet into the cooker, then place the cake tin on top (see Notes). Make sure the tin doesn't touch the water.

6 Lock the lid in place and bring the cooker to high pressure over high heat. Once high pressure is reached, reduce the heat to stabilise the pressure and cook for 20 minutes.

7 Remove the cooker from the heat and release the pressure using the natural release method. Remove the lid carefully. Remove the tin from the cooker (see Notes). Remove the foil from around the tin and bring the cheesecake to room temperature.

8 Refrigerate for 4 hours, or overnight, until well chilled. Cut into wedges to serve.

NOTES: Your pressure cooker needs to be at least 24 cm (9½ inches) wide to hold the cake tin, but it doesn't need to be a 6 litre (210 fl oz) model.

To help get the tin in and out of the cooker, make two foil belts by folding lengths of foil in half continuously until they are 3 cm (1¼ inches) wide. Place the belts on the bench so they form a cross, then place the tin in the centre of the cross. Use the belts to lift the tin into the cooker. Twist the ends of the belts together to form a handle so they won't fall onto the top of the cheesecake.

To make it easier to remove the cheesecake from the tin, turn the base of the tin wrong side up before locking it in place, so that there is no lip around the base of the cheesecake.

Coffee crème caramel

Preparation time 5 minutes (+ overnight chilling) • **Cooking time** 30 minutes • **Serves** 6

375 ml (13 fl oz/1½ cups) milk
375 ml (13 fl oz/1½ cups) pouring (whipping)
cream

45 g (1½ oz/½ cup) espresso coffee beans
295 g (10¼ oz/1⅓ cups) caster (superfine) sugar
6 eggs

1 Put the milk, cream and coffee beans in a saucepan and bring almost to the boil over medium heat. Remove from the heat and stand for 10 minutes to infuse. Strain and discard the beans.

2 Meanwhile, combine 220 g (7¾ oz/1 cup) of the sugar and 125 ml (4 fl oz/½ cup) water in a saucepan over medium heat. Stir until the sugar has dissolved. Increase the heat to high and bring to the boil. Allow to boil, without stirring, for 6–7 minutes, or until the sugar is a deep caramel colour; during cooking, brush down the side of the pan with a pastry brush dipped in water. Pour the caramel into an 18 cm (7 inch) cake tin (see Notes), rotating it so the caramel covers the base and 6 cm (2½ inches) up the side.

3 Whisk the remaining sugar and the eggs in a large bowl until smooth. Stir in the infused milk mixture until combined. Strain into the cake tin, then cover tightly with foil.

4 Pour 250 ml (9 fl oz/1 cup) water into a 6 litre (210 fl oz) pressure cooker. Lower a trivet into the cooker, then place the tin on top (see Notes). Make sure the tin doesn't touch the water.

5 Lock the lid in place and bring the cooker to high pressure over high heat. Once high pressure is reached, reduce the heat to stabilise the pressure and cook for 18 minutes.

6 Remove the cooker from the heat and release the pressure using the natural release method. Remove the lid carefully. Remove the tin from the cooker (see Notes). Remove the foil, then refrigerate the crème caramel overnight.

7 To serve, invert the chilled crème caramel into a deep-sided serving dish and cut into wedges.

NOTES: Use a metal tin rather than a ceramic dish as it will conduct the heat better.

To stop the caramel burning, have a large bowl of cold water ready in which to dip the base of the cake tin when pouring in the caramel. This will cool it down and help set it so it doesn't end up all on the base.

To help lower and remove the cake tin, make two foil belts by folding lengths of foil in half continuously until they are 3 cm (1¼ inches) wide. Place the belts on the bench so they form a cross, then place the tin in the centre of the cross. Use the belts to lift the tin into the cooker. Twist the ends of the belts together to form a handle so they won't fall onto the top of the crème caramel.

The centre of the crème caramel is very wobbly when you remove it from the cooker, but firms up when chilled. The longer you leave the crème caramel to chill before turning it out onto a plate, the more caramel sauce you will get.

Index

Published in 2011 by Murdoch Books Pty Limited

Murdoch Books Australia
Pier 8/9
23 Hickson Road
Millers Point NSW 2000
Phone: +61 (0) 2 8220 2000
Fax: +61 (0) 2 8220 2558
www.murdochbooks.com.au

Murdoch Books UK Limited
Erico House, 6th Floor
93–99 Upper Richmond Road
Putney, London SW15 2TG
Phone: +44 (0) 20 8785 5995
Fax: +44 (0) 20 8785 5985
www.murdochbooks.co.uk

Publisher: Kylie Walker
Designer: Susanne Geppert
Photographer: Natasha Milne
Stylist: Sarah O'Brien
Food Preparation: Brett Sargent
Recipe Development: Lucy Nunes, Brett Sargent, Nick Banbury and the Murdoch Books
Test Kitchen Team
Food Editor: Anneka Manning
Project Editor: Gabriella Sterio
Production: Renee Melbourne

National Library of Australia Cataloguing-in-Publication entry

Title: Quick and Easy Pressure Cooker
ISBN: 978-1-74266-271-8 (hbk.)
Notes: Includes index.
Subjects: Pressure cooking.
                  Quick and easy cooking.
Dewey Number: 641.587

A catalogue record for this book is available from the British Library.

Printed in 2011 by 1010 Printing International Limited, China.

IMPORTANT: Those who might be at risk from the effects of salmonella poisoning (the elderly,
pregnant women, young children and those suffering from immune deficiency diseases) should
consult their doctor with any concerns about eating raw eggs.

OVEN GUIDE: You may find cooking times vary depending on the oven you are using. For fan-
forced ovens, as a general rule, set the oven temperature to 20°C (35°F) lower than indicated
in the recipe.